WALKING THE FIFE PILGRIM WAY

PILGRIMAGE FROM CULROSS AND NORTH QUEENSFERRY TO ST ANDREWS

By Shana Lee Hirsch and Victoria Hunter

JUNIPER HOUSE, MURLEY MOSS,
OXENHOLME ROAD, KENDAL, CUMBRIA LA9 7RL
www.cicerone.co.uk

© Shana Lee Hirsch and Victoria Hunter 2024
First edition 2024
ISBN: 978 1 78631 224 2
eISBN: 978 1 78765 160 9

Printed in Czechia on responsibly sourced paper on behalf of Latitude Press Ltd

A catalogue record for this book is available from the British Library.
All photographs are by the author unless otherwise stated.

© Crown copyright and database rights 2024 OS AC0000810376

UPDATES TO THIS GUIDE

While every effort is made by our authors to ensure the accuracy of guidebooks as they go to print, changes can occur during the lifetime of an edition. Any updates that we know of for this guide will be on the Cicerone website (www.cicerone.co.uk/1224/updates), so please check before planning your trip. We also advise that you check information about such things as transport, accommodation and shops locally. Even rights of way can be altered over time. We are always grateful for information about any discrepancies between a guidebook and the facts on the ground, sent by email to updates@cicerone.co.uk.

Register your book: To sign up to receive free updates, special offers and GPX files where available, create a Cicerone account and register your purchase via the 'My Account' tab at www.cicerone.co.uk.

In memory of Davina Donaldson, our beloved Gran, who showed us the treasures of Fife.

Front cover: St Andrews Cathedral at the end of the Fife Pilgrim Way (Stage 6)

CONTENTS

Overview profile/staging options 4
Route summary table 7
Stage facilities planner 8

INTRODUCTION 13
The Fife Pilgrim Way. 14
Outline of the route 16
A landscape of beliefs. 18

Planning your trip 27
Route options. 27
When to go 27
Getting there and around 29
Accommodation. 29
Refreshments 33
What to bring 33
Children and pets 34

On the trail 35
Using this guide 35
Finding your way 36
Challenges 37

About Fife 38
A brief history. 38
Natural history. 41

THE FIFE PILGRIM WAY 43
Stage 1   Culross to Dunfermline. 45
Stage 1A   North Queensferry to Dunfermline 53
Stage 2   Dunfermline to Kelty. 61
Stage 3   Kelty to Leslie 68
Stage 4   Leslie to Kennoway 75
Stage 5   Kennoway to Ceres 82
Stage 6   Ceres to St Andrews 89

Appendix A   Accommodation. 100
Appendix B   Churches along the FPW 104
Appendix C   Useful contacts. 105
Appendix D   Further reading. 107

WALKING THE FIFE PILGRIM WAY

Overview profile/staging options – Fife Pilgrim Way

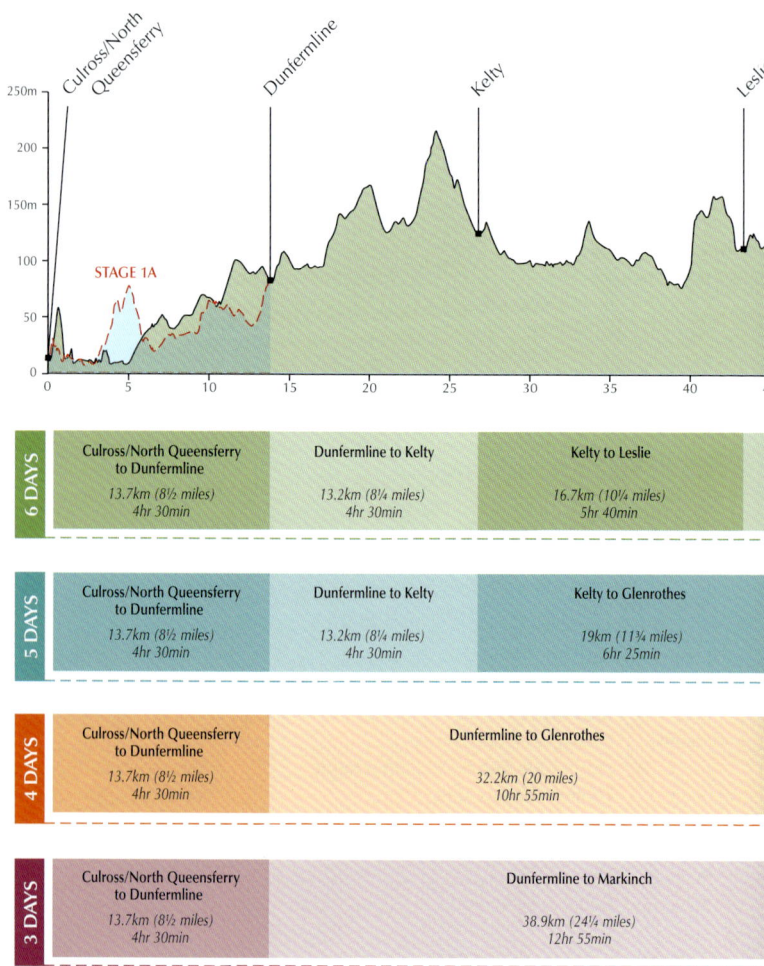

6 DAYS
Culross/North Queensferry to Dunfermline	Dunfermline to Kelty	Kelty to Leslie
13.7km (8½ miles) *4hr 30min*	*13.2km (8¼ miles)* *4hr 30min*	*16.7km (10¼ miles)* *5hr 40min*

5 DAYS
Culross/North Queensferry to Dunfermline	Dunfermline to Kelty	Kelty to Glenrothes
13.7km (8½ miles) *4hr 30min*	*13.2km (8¼ miles)* *4hr 30min*	*19km (11¾ miles)* *6hr 25min*

4 DAYS
Culross/North Queensferry to Dunfermline	Dunfermline to Glenrothes
13.7km (8½ miles) *4hr 30min*	*32.2km (20 miles)* *10hr 55min*

3 DAYS
Culross/North Queensferry to Dunfermline	Dunfermline to Markinch
13.7km (8½ miles) *4hr 30min*	*38.9km (24¼ miles)* *12hr 55min*

Overview profile/staging options

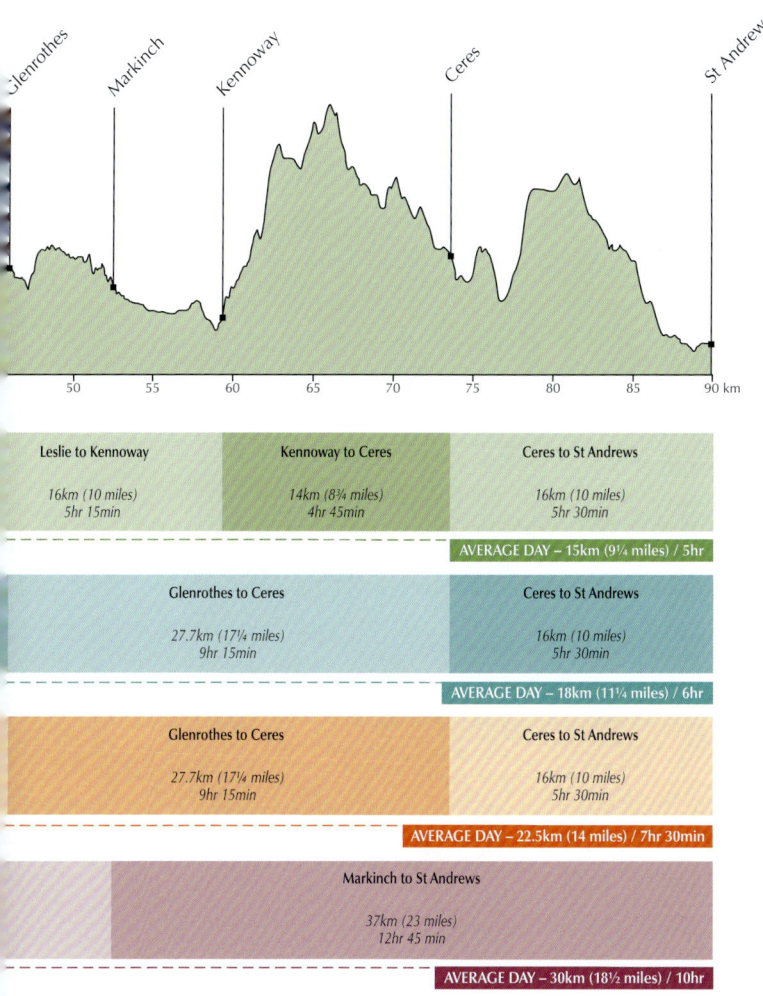

Leslie to Kennoway	Kennoway to Ceres	Ceres to St Andrews
16km (10 miles) 5hr 15min	14km (8¾ miles) 4hr 45min	16km (10 miles) 5hr 30min

AVERAGE DAY – 15km (9¼ miles) / 5hr

Glenrothes to Ceres	Ceres to St Andrews
27.7km (17¼ miles) 9hr 15min	16km (10 miles) 5hr 30min

AVERAGE DAY – 18km (11¼ miles) / 6hr

Glenrothes to Ceres	Ceres to St Andrews
27.7km (17¼ miles) 9hr 15min	16km (10 miles) 5hr 30min

AVERAGE DAY – 22.5km (14 miles) / 7hr 30min

Markinch to St Andrews
37km (23 miles) 12hr 45 min

AVERAGE DAY – 30km (18½ miles) / 10hr

The New Abbey portion of Dunfermline Abbey with 'KING ROBERT THE BRUCE' atop it (Stage 1 and 1A)

ROUTE SUMMARY TABLE

Stage	Start	Finish	Time	Distance (km)	Distance (miles)	Ascent (m)	Descent (m)
1	Culross	Dunfermline	4hr 30min	13.7	8½	180	105
1A	North Queensferry	Dunfermline	4hr 30min	13.7	8½	210	130
2	Dunfermline	Kelty	4hr 30min	13.2	8¼	210	170
3	Kelty	Leslie	5hr 40min	16.7	10¼	170	175
4	Leslie	Kennoway	5hr 15min	16	10	100	150
5	Kennoway	Ceres	4hr 45min	14	8¾	240	235
6	Ceres	St Andrews	5hr 30min	16	10	170	230
Totals main route			30hr 10min	89.6km	55¾ miles	1280m	1195m

Route symbols on OS map extracts
(for OS legend see printed OS maps)

route
alternative route
start point
finish point
route direction

SCALE: 1:50,000

0 kilometres 0.5 1
0 miles   0.5

Features on the overview map

 urban area

 national park
eg **CAIRNGORMS**

 forest park/national forest
eg *Tay Forest Park*

 National Scenic Area
eg *Cuillin Hills*

GPX files for all routes can be downloaded free at www.cicerone.co.uk/1224/GPX.

WALKING THE FIFE PILGRIM WAY

STAGE FACILITIES PLANNER

Stage	Place	Walking time	Cum. stage time	Distance (km)	Cum. stage distance (km)
1	**Culross**	-	-	-	-
1	Cairneyhill	2hr 40min	2hr 40min	8km	8km
1	Crossford	50min	3 hr 30min	2.5km	10.5km
2	**Dunfermline**	**1hr**	**4hr 30min**	**3.2km**	**13.7km**
1A	**North Queensferry**	-	-	-	-
1A	Inverkeithing	1hr 20min	1hr 20min	4km	4km
1A	Rosyth	40min	2hr	2.5km	6.5km
2	**Dunfermline**	**2hr 30min**	**4hr 30min**	**7.2km**	**13.7km**
2	*Craigduckie/Loch Fitty*	+40min/2km off route			
2	Kingseat	2hr	2hr	5.5km	5.5km
2, 3	*Kinross*	+3hr 30min/10km off route			
3	**Kelty**	**2hr 30min**	**4hr 30min**	**7.7km**	**13.2km**
3	Lochore Meadows Country Park	20min	20min	1km	1km
3	*Lochgelly*	+40min/2km off route			
3	Crosshill	1hr 20min	1hr 40min	4km	5km
3	*Cardenden*	+20min/0.8km off route			
3	Kinglassie	2hr 30min	4hr 10min	7.5km	12.5km
4	**Leslie**	**1hr 30min**	**5hr 40min**	**4.2km**	**16.7km**
4	Glenrothes	45min	45min	2km	2km
4	Balfarg	1hr 15min	2hr	3.7km	5.7km
4	Balbirnie	30min	2hr 30min	1.6km	7.3km

Stage Facilities Planner

◯ Hotel ◯ B&B/guesthouse ◯ Self-catering (including pods/glamping)

◉ Bus ◉ Train 🍴 Refreshments ⊕ Grocery shop ⊞ ATM ✪ Outdoor shop

Hotel	B&B	Self-catering	Refreshments	Grocery	Outdoor	Train	Bus	ATM
	B&B	SC	🍴				Bus	
H			🍴	Gro			Bus	ATM
H			🍴	Gro			Bus	ATM
H	B&B		🍴	Gro	Out	Train	Bus	ATM
H		SC	🍴	Gro		Train	Bus	ATM
			🍴	Gro		Train	Bus	ATM
H	B&B		🍴	Gro		Train	Bus	ATM
H	B&B		🍴	Gro	Out	Train	Bus	ATM
		SC						
							Bus	
H			🍴	Gro			Bus	ATM
			🍴	Gro			Bus	ATM
			🍴				Bus	
				Gro		Train	Bus	ATM
				Gro				
			🍴			Train	Bus	ATM
			🍴	Gro			Bus	
H	B&B		🍴	Gro			Bus	ATM
H			🍴	Gro	Out	Train	Bus	ATM
H								
H			🍴					

WALKING THE FIFE PILGRIM WAY

Stage	Place	Walking time	Cum. stage time	Distance (km)	Cum. stage distance (km)
4	Markinch	15min	2hr 45min	1.2km	8.5km
4	Windygates	2hr	4hr 45min	6km	14.5km
4, 5	Leven	+1hr 30min/5km off route			
5	**Kennoway**	**30min**	**5h 15min**	**1.5km**	**16km**
5	Clatto Reservoir	2hr 50min	2hr 50min	8.5km	8.5km
6	**Ceres**	**1hr 55min**	**4hr 45min**	**5.5km**	**14km**
6	Craigtoun Park	3hr 45min	3hr 45min	11km	11km
6	**St Andrews**	**1hr 45min**	**5hr 30min**	**5km**	**16km**

St Andrews Castle with the West Sands in the background (Stage 6)

STAGE FACILITIES PLANNER

Facilities

The Way cuts through a small forest (Stage 6)

INTRODUCTION

A peaceful bench beside the FPW looking over the Cairnsmill Burn (Stage 6)

The Fife Pilgrim Way (FPW) traverses the heart of the Kingdom of Fife, in central Scotland. In addition to significant historical and religious places, you will visit important industrial and mining complexes, rich farmlands that have been tended for millennia, and places that diverse people now call home. Whether you walk one kilometre or one hundred, you will experience a landscape steeped in history from ancient times to modern day. This experience will change you, deepening your connection to this place, and that is what the adventure of walking the Fife Pilgrim Way is all about: connection to the age-old yet ever-changing land of Fife.

The Fife Pilgrim Way is both old and new. Officially opened in 2019, it is the latest waymarked pilgrim route to St Andrews. Yet its recent opening does not mean that it is a new pilgrim route. People have been walking across Fife to St Andrews since the mediaeval era, travelling on foot from around the UK to some of the most important pilgrimage sites in Western Europe, including the shrines of St Margaret and St Andrew.

In this guide, the term 'pilgrim' is used in a diverse sense. A 'pilgrim' is any person going on a journey with intention. You do not need to be on a spiritual quest to become a pilgrim. If pilgrimages are not your thing at all,

WALKING THE FIFE PILGRIM WAY

A first glimpse of the end destination of St Andrews is visible from the golf course by Craigtoun Country Park (Stage 6)

that's OK, too. You do not have to be a pilgrim to walk the Fife Pilgrim Way. This route can be undertaken by anyone, whether or not they are interested in visiting ancient and holy sites. There are rich experiences awaiting everyone on this path – from birdlife and hidden wild places, to witnessing the history of mining and the economic changes that have occurred across the centuries, to stones from prehistoric times, to the farming communities that have tilled the fertile soil for centuries. Many kinds of people have walked these same routes, and now, you too are invited.

THE FIFE PILGRIM WAY

Although there are several long-distance paths that arrive in St Andrews, the Fife Pilgrim Way offers an alternative to the windswept and popular Fife Coastal Path. Walking the Fife Pilgrim Way lets you experience a lesser known, quieter, yet equally stunning part of rural Scotland, all the while passing through centuries of history. Fife is a true pilgrims' kingdom, and this new route allows you to travel through the centre of this kingdom.

Long-distance walking, and pilgrimage in particular, has been undergoing a recent revival. In part, this is

THE FIFE PILGRIM WAY

due to organisations such as the British Pilgrimage Trust (BPT), which exists to 'advance British pilgrimage as a form of cultural heritage that promotes holistic wellbeing, for the public benefit'. The BPT specifically promotes pilgrimage as an inclusive and accessible practice that reflects the diversity of Britain today. There are several reasons why more people are opting for long-distance walking as a form of exploration and travel; walking has health benefits, is low-impact and low-carbon, it is economical, and it is a way of exploring landscapes that often go unseen from roads and railways.

The Fife Coast & Countryside Trust (FCCT), an official charity, are the official caretakers of most of the trail system that makes up the FPW. The FCCT have been maintaining the highly successful Fife Coastal Path for over twenty years. Building on this success, the FPW made good sense as the next long-distance path for the organisation. While the Fife Coastal Path brings thousands of walkers to the coastal areas of Fife each year, the interior of the region is less visited, and some may say neglected. The revival of the FPW addresses this coastal bias.

Further, much of what now forms the FPW has been a pilgrim route for centuries. The most popular phase, between the 11th and 16th centuries, saw thousands of pilgrims travelling across Fife to St Andrews Cathedral and the shrine of St Margaret in Dunfermline. In addition to these age-old religious pilgrim routes, walkers today can also witness centuries of rich cultural and material histories on the journey.

One of the special waymarkers in the ground (Stage 1A)

Dunfermline Abbey is visible beyond fields of crops (Stage 1)

Although the modern FPW officially launched in July 2019, efforts to recreate the way have been ongoing for many years. A grassroots group of local churches, history organisations, academic experts and others, created the Scottish Pilgrim Routes Forum and the Fife Pilgrim Way Network in 2012. With the support of Fife Council, Fife Tourism Partnership and funding from the National Lottery and the European Commission's rural development, or LEADER programme, the route became reality.

OUTLINE OF THE ROUTE

The route has two alternative starting points: Stage 1 departs from Culross, and Stage 1A leaves from North Queensferry. Each are equally beautiful walks, and it is impossible to recommend one over the other. If you begin in Culross (Stage 1), you will experience one of the most complete villages, or 'burghs' from the 17th century, and have the opportunity to visit the evocative Culross Palace and gardens. Exploring the tiny cobbled streets and historic sites of Culross can

OUTLINE OF THE ROUTE

easily take a day. Alternatively, if you begin in North Queensferry (Stage 1A), you will be starting at the location where mediaeval pilgrims landed after crossing the Firth of Forth on the 'Queen's Ferry', named after Queen Margaret. Today, you will be starting at the foot of the Forth Rail Bridge, a UNESCO World Heritage Site. On this stage, you also pass through Inverkeithing, which once hosted pilgrims in its Franciscan 'Hospitium', which still stands today.

Whichever starting stage you choose, Dunfermline is the first city you will encounter, and it is a touchstone of the route. It was once home to Scotland's monarchs and contains what remains of a Benedictine Abbey as well as the ruins of the royal palace.

Stage 2 departs from Dunfermline heading north to Kingseat and Kelty, entering the heart of Fife's mining heritage and the legacy landscape of this important industry.

Stage 3 departs again from the village of Kelty, and travels through Lochore Meadows Country Park, where you can witness the restoration of a mining landscape into a place of recreation and birdlife. Passing through the former mining village of Kinglassie brings you to a rare treat – Finglassin's Well, a restored holy well for passing pilgrims.

Stage 4 picks up where Stage 3 ends, in the suburb of Leslie, outside the 'new town' of Glenrothes, with a walk along the River Leven, where

The recently restored Finglassin's Well (Stage 3)

mills used to flourish in the 1800s. While Glenrothes is a modern town, built after World War 2, it is still interwoven with the past. Indeed, you will walk through two neolithic sites, the stone circles of Balfarg and Balbirnie, bringing the stone age into a modern residential landscape. The mediaeval town of Markinch with a parish church tower from the 12th Century, dedicated to St Drostan, is also on the way, before the stage ends in the small town of Kennoway.

Stage 5 is the most remote and isolated part of the way, rising through the quiet countryside to Clatto Hill, the highest point, before descending through fields and woodlands into the market town of Ceres, the start of Stage 6. After a stop at the Fife Folk Museum at the picturesque town

The West Port welcomes pilgrims into historic St Andrews (Stage 6)

centre, crossing Bishops Bridge will take you onwards to the Waterless Way, and deep into the Fife countryside. You will be walking an ancient road, where travellers and pilgrims have passed for centuries. This peaceful stage finally takes you into the coastal town of St Andrews, where you can explore its fascinating history, and take in the bustling university town with its many boutiques, restaurants, beach walks, and, of course, golf. Indeed, the reasons for making a pilgrimage to the tourist hot-spot of St Andrews are many, both in the past, and today.

A LANDSCAPE OF BELIEFS

In mediaeval times, people went on pilgrimages for different reasons: as acts of devotion, as penance to seek God's forgiveness, or to visit a saint's relics in search of healing and power. This landscape of saints is still written in the parishes and holy sites across Fife. Yet there are more ancient beliefs still visible on the landscape today. People in the Neolithic period (c. 3500BC) built monumental henges, standing stones, and chambered tombs, some of which can be seen along the route. Similarly, Bronze Age inhabitants of Fife (c. 2500BC) continued to use these structures and transformed them to meet their own uses and belief systems. Iron Age (c. 700BC) hillforts and crannogs are also found along the route. While the meaning of these monuments and the spiritualities of the people who lived then are lost to time, they serve as a connective thread to a common humanity seeking meaning.

Celtic beliefs

During the early centuries AD, Celtic and Pictish tribes battled to keep the Romans from moving north into what is now Scotland. St Ninian, born in what is now Scotland around AD360, founded a monastery at Whithorn around AD420. In AD563, Colum Cille, who eventually became Saint Columba, arrived in Iona from Ireland to establish his famous monastery. The Celtic and Pictish tribes of Scotland likely gradually incorporated Christian rituals and beliefs into their own pagan religions. This is evident in many of the pre-Christian festivals such as Beltane (May Day), which modern Christian holy days often coincide with, including Samhain (All Hallow's Eve). These festivals are still celebrated by many people in Scotland today. This amalgamation of pagan and early Christian beliefs is also evident in many of the stone carvings from this era, when pagan and Christian motifs and symbols were often combined in non-confrontational ways.

Stob Cross, a Pictish stone, outside of Markinch (Stage 4)

The early years of Christianity in Scotland are surprisingly visible in Fife, as it was a destination of many early Celtic Christian pilgrims, monks and missionaries. The ancient Celtic Church, also known as the Culdees or *Céile Dé*, which means 'companions of God' in Gaelic, were particularly active in Fife. Although little is definitively known about them, the *Céile Dé* were a Christian monastic community that spanned the British Isles, including Ireland during the Middle Ages. Many of them were likely lay people, and even abbots married.

Culross Abbey Church (Stage 1)

They lived in monastic-style communities that were sometimes connected to cathedrals, but situated outside of them. There were known Culdee communities at Loch Leven, St Andrews, Markinch, Kirkaldy, and other locations across Fife.

The details of the Culdee beliefs and way of life are somewhat lost to folkloric oral history, but they likely combined some early, Druidic beliefs, and transferred some Celtic pagan gods, such as Bridgid, into Saints. While some Culdees eventually joined the Roman Catholic church, many of them moved out of the public eye, and the historybooks, by the 1300s. Despite the lack of historical detail, the Culdees played an important role in creating the uniquely Celtic Christian culture and beliefs of Scotland.

Catholicism and the Reformation

Benedictine abbeys began to be established in the 11th century with the first in Dunfermline around 1070. These orders included Cistertian, Augustinian, and Benedictine. Augustinians were located at St Andrews, alongside the Culdees by the 1300s. In the 11th century, Queen Margaret and King Malcolm III forwarded a movement to put the church in Scotland under increasing Roman authority through the establishment of monasteries. During the Mediaeval period in Scotland, the cult of saints proliferated (see The cult of saints in Fife, below) and many monasteries flourished as Roman Catholicism was the dominant order.

The Scottish Reformation began with reformation-related violence from the early 1400s. Reformers' beliefs were influenced by humanists such as Erasmus, whose works they encountered as scholars at the university. Tensions continued to build into the early 1500s, and St Andrews became a hotspot for Reformation ideas. This was, in part, due to its position as the seat of the Catholic Church in Scotland, but the university was also a harbour for continental ideas, where the reformist thought of leaders such as Martin Luther and John Calvin were able to circulate. A full-blown riot followed a sermon from John Knox in 1559, which resulted in St Andrews Cathedral being sacked and burned. Several outspoken upper-class Protestants were also executed during the Reformation violence, including Patrick Hamilton and George Wishart, whose death by burning led to the killing of Cardinal David Beaton at St Andrews Castle.

After these events, Knox and other Protestants were exiled to Europe, and upon returning, Knox, who had become a follower of Calvin, was able to influence a series of royal alliances and the adoption of Presbyterianism by the nobles. By 1560, the Scottish Parliament broke from the papacy and declared Protestantism to be the religion of the state.

The Reformation had a strong impact on Scotland's culture, including the reorganisation of governance structures, destruction of many of the cathedrals, and a shift in all aspects of culture, including art, music, and education. The Kirk, or Scottish Church, and the local parish system came to influence both worship and daily lives. Unlike the Reformation in England, however, there was not wide-spread, systematic persecution, although several lairds and nobles were executed violently, mainly in St Andrews. Similarly, the monasteries were not immediately dissolved, as they were elsewhere in England and Wales, and instead allowed to slowly die out. Roman Catholicism was officially illegal, but continued to exist in parts of Scotland, although mostly in individual homes.

Persecution of witches

Although the Scottish Reformation was a violent time, and people were brutally killed, there is a much less-considered period of violence that was ushered in with the passage of the Witchcraft Act of 1563. Across Scotland, an estimated 3837 people, mostly women, were accused of witchcraft. It is also estimated that around 2558 people were tortured and murdered by the church and state, the torture serving to elicit confessions.

Although a similar scenario was happening in other parts of Europe, Scotland played a huge role in the number of people killed as witches. Women were not able to provide testimony at their trial. Many of those who died were poor, or considered outsiders or independent thinkers. The Witchcraft Act was in force until 1736.

Today there is a nationwide campaign, 'Witches of Scotland', which is seeking a pardon, an apology, and a national memorial to those that were killed. They were successful in fulfilling part of their demand when, in 2022, then First Minister Nicola Sturgeon formally apologised and acknowledged the 'egregious, historic injustice' and 'deep misogyny' that led to the murder of so many women. The campaign for a formal monument continues, although there are several smaller monuments along the FPW, an effort of the local community to commemorate these unthinkable events.

Religion and spirituality in Fife today

Some may say that Scotland as a whole is going through another time of religious change, as the population moves away from formal religion. As of 2021, the census found that 61% of residents in Fife say that they have no religion, significantly higher than the national average. Religion in Scotland is changing, but not going away. One-fifth of Scots identify with the Church of Scotland, and 13% as Roman Catholic, and there are growing populations of Muslims, Buddhists, Hindus, Sikhs, and Neo-Pagans across all of Scotland.

THE PILGRIM PASTOR

The Church of Scotland and the Episcopal Church have funded and appointed a 'Pilgrim Pastor', Rev. Duncan Weaver, whose job is to get people out walking the FPW. He regularly leads short walks and even full-length pilgrimages, and invites people of all fitness levels, and of any faith or none to join. He is also working to establish a system whereby pilgrims may stay at historic churches along the way. More information can be found under 'Accommodation' and in Appendix B.

His website is https://fifecoastandcountrysidetrust.co.uk/projects/the-pilgrim-pastor

The cult of saints in Fife

Saint Margaret

Queen Margaret, or Saint Margaret as she would come to be known, is an important character in the story of the Fife Pilgrim Way. Margaret was not only a saint, but an important historical figure in Scotland. She was of royal English descent, but was born in Hungary around 1045, eventually marrying King Malcolm III of Scotland after escaping to Dunfermline for safety after the Battle of Hastings.

St Margaret and King Malcolm III had eight children, and three of them became kings of Scotland. Together, they built Scotland's first Benedictine monastery along with the original church at Dunfermline. Margaret also revived Iona's monastery and supported the construction of St Rule's tower in St Andrews. She is considered famous for her extreme devotion and prayer, as well as her generosity. It is said that she would serve dinner to the poor before eating, supposedly up to three-hundred people at one time.

Her last years were brutal. When her husband and son were killed by the Earl of Northumbria in Northern England, she is said to have died of grief three days later on 16 November, 1093, age 48. She and her husband were buried at Dunfermline Abbey. She became Saint Margaret around 1250, when she was canonised by Pope Innocent IV, on account of over 45 miracles.

North Queensferry was chosen as an appropriate starting point for the Fife Pilgrim Way because of its significance for pilgrims past. Established by Margaret, North Queensferry was, for pilgrims on their way to St Andrews, the first point they would reach after crossing the Forth Estuary. In Dunfermline, you will encounter St Margaret, and you will be walking the pilgrimage path of thousands of others through the ages, especially those honouring St Margaret by visiting her relics at Dunfermline Abbey. It could be argued that the Fife Pilgrim Way is St Margaret's Way, but the stories of other saints also come alive along the route.

Saint Andrew

Andrew is well known as the patron saint of Scotland, and this promotion occurred in the mid 10th century. An important figure to Christians globally, he was one of the 12 apostles of Christ, and the brother of St Peter. He is also called the 'first Apostle' because he was a follower of John the Baptist. A shrine at St Andrews Cathedral once held his relics, prompting pilgrims from around the UK and Europe to visit the town by the thousands.

There are many legends, in many different countries, that posit special meaning to St Andrew. Some ancient manuscripts state that Andrew's relics were brought by Pictish king, Óengus Mac Fergusa, to St Andrews. The Saltire (flag of Scotland), has a representation of St Andrew's cross, and is said to be based on a vision of the Pictish King Angus, who prayed to St Andrew to protect his army in battle in AD832. The morning of the battle, the story goes, he saw a cross of clouds in the form of an X in the sky above him. He saw this cross as representing the crucifix upon which Andrew was killed, and declared Andrew the patron saint of Scotland after winning the battle against the Angles. This symbol has since become the flag of Scotland – a white cross set against a blue sky. St Andrews will be a place to remember and connect with this saint.

Saint Kentigern (Mungo)
Saint Kentigern, or Saint Mungo as he is known in Scotland, is Glasgow's patron saint. He was born in the mid-6th century to Saint Theneva (Teneu). When Theneva, a princess, was found to be pregnant, she was thrown from a hill into the Firth of Forth by her father. Fortunately, she landed in a boat, which brought her across to Culross, where the monks took care of her. There, she gave birth to St Mungo, one of the only Scottish-born mediaeval saint-missionaries (most are from Ireland). He was raised by Saint Serf, and is credited with building the first church in Glasgow, which is now the location of the Cathedral.

Saint Mungo is still one of the most honoured of the Scottish saints. He is said to have completed four miracles in Glasgow, including bringing a robin back to life after his classmates had killed it. His birthplace is found along the FPW just outside of Culross at a somewhat forgotten ruin of a chapel. He probably died in AD603, and was buried in Glasgow Cathedral, where it is said his remains still lay. Culross is a place to connect with St Mungo, as you pass his birthplace on the Firth of Forth.

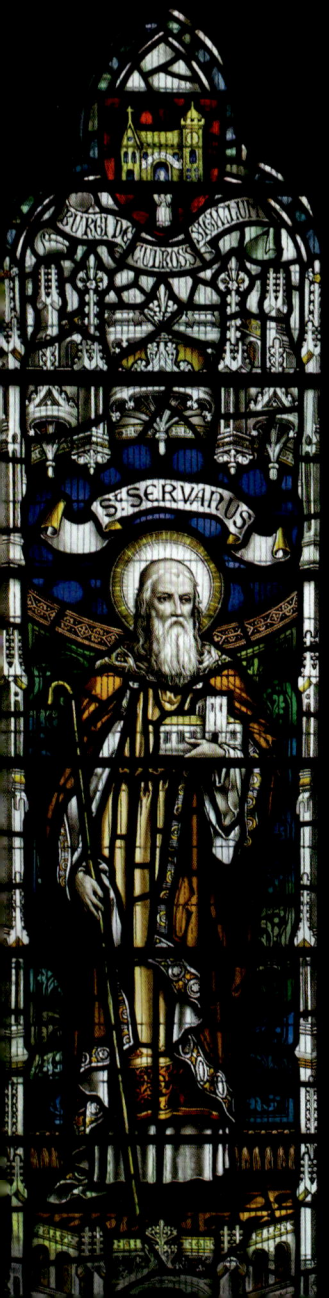

Saint Serf (Serbán)

Saint Serf, or Serbán, is particularly venerated in Fife. Legend says that he was born to the King of Canaan and a princess of Arabia sometime around AD500, and at one point served the Pope in Rome. He travelled to Scotland and was shown an island in Loch Leven by the then abbot of Iona, Adomnán. He established St Serf's Inch Priory on this island, which became an Augustinian priory. He is also said to have established the priory at Culross, where he raised Saint Kentigern. It is claimed that he committed miracles across Fife and beyond, including slaying a dragon in Strathearn, just to the north of Fife. According to legend, he was buried at Culross sometime around AD583. While you are in Culross, you will encounter places that echo his presence, such as the Abbey.

Other saints in Fife

Several other saints are often mentioned in places along the FPW. These include Saint Drostan, usually associated with Northeast Scotland. St Drostan's tower is located in Markinch. Saint Kenneth is venerated in Kennoway, where Kennoway Parish Church was dedicated in the late 12th Century. St Kenneth, or Cainneach of Aghaboe, was a mediaeval Irish missionary who lived from about AD515–600, and was a friend of St Columba. The Kennoway Den, along the burn to the west of the village, has a cave that was said to be where St Kenneth lived and prayed.

PLANNING YOUR TRIP

Pilgrims follow the trail towards Kelty (Stage 2)

ROUTE OPTIONS

There are several staging options available, which you can choose between, based on the pace you would like to take. What may be considered a more leisurely pace is preferred, completing, on average, under 15km a day. This is still a challenging walk, but not too strenuous. This also avoids rushing, and with stops along the way to check out sites, have a picnic, or stop for tea and treats, this pace seems about right. Walking at this pace will give you a six-day itinerary. The alternative schedules provide options for 5-, 4-, and 3-day journeys. Choose the one that is the right pace for you.

WHEN TO GO

The weather in Fife is similar to the rest of the British Isles. Being influenced by its maritime situation, it is much warmer than its latitude would suggest. Fife is generally more sunny and drier than most of Scotland. Average rainfall is around 700–900mm per year, with rain being fairly evenly spread out across the year. Month to month, the chance of rainy weather is not markedly different, although February to June is generally (only slightly) drier, with 48–67mm of rain per month, than July to January, with an average of 71–86mm per month. The wettest month is statistically

A pilgrim walks along the B9037, beside Torry Burn (Stage 1)

October, although climate change is making this more difficult to predict, and there have recently been years with summer droughts.

Temperatures are generally mild, with a mean daily maximum of 6°C in January, and 18°C in July. Winds are usually from the south-west, and can be strong at times, especially in more open areas and higher elevations, as in the rest of Scotland. This is one reason why walking the route from south-west to north-east is a good idea; most likely, you will have the wind at your back. It should be noted that the winter can bring strong and unpredictable storms, including gales and heavy snow, especially in the higher elevations, which could make some of the hills impassable on foot for short periods.

So, 'when is the best time to walk the FPW?' In answer to this question, it might be most important to consider the length of the day. Since the weather can encompass 'four seasons in a day' in Fife, consider instead the hours of daylight. The longest day of the year, June 21st, has 17 hours and 41 minutes of daylight, whereas the shortest, Dec 21st, has only 6 hours and 53 minutes! For many of the stages, you'd have to be walking from dawn until dusk in the winter, which may not be very pleasant. The best time to walk the way is therefore probably from about April until September, when the weather is the mildest, and the daylight is the longest. Springtime and early summer are a particularly magical time in Scotland, as the land comes alive again after the darkness of winter and the spring lambs are born. The long days end with a seemingly never-ending twilight for the weeks leading up to and around the Summer Solstice, and it can feel luxurious to spend these days outside.

GETTING THERE AND AROUND

Getting to the terminuses: Edinburgh is the nearest major terminus for inward travel via road, rail, or air. International travellers may also need to fly to London before finding transport connections to Scotland. Trains and buses are recommended. There are many trains each day to the start of Stage 1A in North Queensferry. If you are starting in Culross, at Stage 1, you will need to take a bus to the starting point. At the end of the FPW in St Andrews, there is a bus station with transport to Edinburgh, or to Leuchars, the nearest train station.

Fife has an excellent public transport network. Traveline (www.traveline.info) will help you find the buses and trains that you will need to get to the start or end of each of the stages. Between start and end terminus, Stage 1 is served by bus, Stage 1A by bus or train (if you use Dunfermline Queen Margaret Station), and Stage 2 is served by bus. Stages 3 and 4 will require taking two buses, so a taxi may be preferred. Both stages 5 and 6 are served by one bus. If you do not want to through-walk the entire Way, but instead complete it in sections over time, it is possible to park at the end of each stage and take a bus, train, or taxi to the start, walking back towards your vehicle (or vice versa).

Taxis are fairly inexpensive and asking for the local taxi service number in a local shop is usually a good way to get a quick lift. Buses generally run fairly frequently, but in some of the more rural areas there may be large gaps between services. The schedule for both buses and trains is usually abbreviated on weekends, especially Sundays. Night buses can be rare, so keep an eye on the timetables and don't necessarily expect a bus to be running beyond regular business hours. Again, checking with Traveline will help.

ACCOMMODATION

There are several options for accommodation, depending on your budget and the type of adventure you would like to have. It is possible to walk the FPW from stage to stage and wild camp all along the way. Another option is to stay in accommodation such as hotels and B&Bs each night. In some areas, accommodation can be costly so it is advisable to look into all options. Some short-term holiday lets such as self-catering accommodation and homestays (Airbnb, for example) are not listed in Appendix A because they prefer more than one night's stay. There may also be opportunities to stay in local churches along the way, or 'Champ' (Church-camp), and more information is provided

WALKING THE FIFE PILGRIM WAY

CONTINUING YOUR JOURNEY

The FPW does not have to be the end of your pilgrimage. You can continue on to follow several other long-distance waymarked routes that converge in St Andrews. These include:

- The Fife Coastal Path (FCP), which runs for 187km (116 miles) along the coast of Fife from Kincardine in the south to Newburgh in the north. The route runs through St Andrews, so you could extend your FPW walk in either direction, heading north and then west for another 38.5km (24 miles) to Newburgh. Alternatively, you could turn south through the picturesque fishing villages of Fife to create a circular route with an additional 98km (61 miles) to North Queensferry or 118km/73¼ miles to Culross. There is a wide variety of accommodation all along the coast, and the route is popular with long-distance and day-walkers alike.
- St Margaret's Way loops to the south from St Andrews, either along the coast, following the FCP, or through the countryside. It then follows the FCP back to Edinburgh. The total route is 98km (61 miles) and was inspired by St Margaret. It is not as well established as the other routes, but because you will be following the FCP and FPW, it is fairly well marked by those paths.
- St Duthac's Way heads north from St Andrews for 156km (97 miles) to Aberdeen. It follows a gorgeous coastline and passes several important historic sites such as Arbroath Abbey and Dunnottar Castle.
- For an epic journey, travel towards Iona on St Columba's Way. This route takes you from St Andrews to the Isle of Iona (or vice versa). The total walk is 420km (261 miles) and traverses the breadth of Scotland and the Isle of Mull. Some parts of this trail are truly remote.

in Appendix B. Make sure you call ahead to discuss options for staying in local churches, as these opportunities are still in development.

If you plan to stay in B&Bs, guesthouses or hotels, you should be aware that some stages have sparse to no accommodation. Thus, extra planning is necessary for the stages that start or end in Kelty and Kennoway. This usually means taking a short taxi or bus to a nearby town where accommodation is available. This should not be a problem, however, as the neighbouring towns are only a few kilometres off-route. Detailed information is provided in each stage. If you are willing to walk the route at a faster pace than is laid out in the stage chapters in this book, you can avoid this situation (as outlined in the alternative schedules). If you are staying in B&Bs, hotels, or

ACCOMMODATION

similar accommodation, you should book well ahead of time. Be aware that in the summer accommodation can book up many months in advance.

Note that some of the recommended accommodation states a **minimum number of nights per stay**, but when asked, can often accommodate people walking the FPW. It is worth calling and mentioning that is your intention, and they may allow you to stay only one night.

Wild camping

Thanks to the Scottish Outdoor Access Code, wild camping is legal in Scotland. In contrast to England and Wales, in Scotland you have legal access rights to be on any land as long as you behave responsibly. You can access most places using this code, with some common-sense exceptions including houses and gardens, land where crops are growing, school grounds, etc.

This free access includes camping, which can make walking a long-distance route such as this very relaxing, since you do not have to arrive at any particular destination at a specific time – you can just find a reasonable site and set up your tent. Keep in mind, however, that some areas of the FPW pass through urban town centres, and you may not want to camp near them so as to avoid being bothered by noise or other people. The towns you pass through are generally fairly small, however, so you would be able to walk to the edge and find countryside reasonably quickly and easily. You do not need to ask permission to camp on someone's land, but if you do see someone who looks responsible for the land, you can ask them if they have any suggestions of where to camp out of the way. Be respectful and aware of your surroundings.

As the path takes you alongside fields, Dunfermline is visible in the distance (Stage 1A)

WALKING THE FIFE PILGRIM WAY

RESPONSIBLE WILD CAMPING

'Behaving responsibly' means following the Scottish Outdoor Access Code (SOAC):
- Respect the interests of others
- Care for the environment
- Take responsibility for your own actions

Some things to keep in mind when wild camping include:
- Follow advice from land managers
- Do not create an obstruction
- Leave gates as you find them
- Keep to unsown ground, field edges, paths
- Camp away from buildings and roads
- Leave no trace of your campsite
- Bring a trowel to bury your waste, and urinate away from water

For full details of the SOAC, see www.outdooraccess-scotland.scot.

The high street in Dunfermline contains many useful shops for gear and food (Stage 2)

Champing

Camping in churches, or 'champing' as it is also known, may be a further option. While, as of publication, there is no formal arrangement with the churches along the Way, there is an active effort to create a system whereby those walking the FPW can sleep inside the parish churches along the route. Many churches along the Way are involved in this effort, and there may be formal options in the near future. In the meantime, it is worth contacting the churches and asking them if they would be willing to support your journey with overnight accommodation. Keep in mind that this accommodation would involve bringing your own camping gear such as a sleeping bag and pad, and that you would likely be sleeping on a floor or pew inside a dry, but possibly cold building.

Nevertheless, this would be an exciting development for the FPW, and for those looking to have a unique pilgrim experience. Most of the churches along or close to the route that have websites are listed in Appendix B. Please make sure you contact the churches and ask about the current status of their participation in the programme beforehand.

REFRESHMENTS

Most towns and villages have all you will need to stock up on picnic supplies and water. There are also many cafes, pubs, and restaurants that you can stop at for some rest and refreshment. At the start of each stage, there is an overview of what is available along the route. Most (but not all) cafes and restaurants cater to those with food sensitivities and allergies, and will have gluten-free, nut-free, vegetarian and vegan options. Each small town usually has at least one small shop with basic food, beverage, and other supplies, and many have a small grocery store such as a Coop that will have 'grab and go' sandwiches and snacks for a reasonable price. Larger towns such as Glenrothes, St Andrews and Dunfermline have many large grocery chains.

You will want to be wary of some longer stretches in the later stages, where there can be several kilometres between facilities. Make sure to carry your own water, as it is not safe to drink from natural water sources.

WHAT TO BRING

Bring layers and dress for the season. It is a good idea to always carry a waterproof jacket and trousers, as it can rain at any time and showers are common. An extra pair of dry socks is often nice to have. You will likely want a warm but lightweight jacket, and in all but the hottest weather a warm hat and possibly gloves. If walking in summer, a sun hat and sunscreen could be necessary. Insect repellent will keep biting flies and ticks away. Make sure to bring plenty of water and food, especially on the longer stretches. Trekking poles may not be helpful or needed because much of the ground is gravel or paved, but collapsible poles could come in handy. Essentials for emergencies include maps, compass, whistle, torch, and a first aid kit with bandages and plasters for blisters. Some optional items include: binoculars and/or field guides for birding. Bring some petty cash and change if you plan to take a bus, although you can also purchase tickets online.

If you are walking the route over multiple days, make sure to bring all you will need including a pack towel and toiletries. If you are camping, you will need to carry your bedding as well as your tent, and possibly a stove for warm meals. If you are staying at hotel or guesthouse accommodation, you will not need to bring towels or bedding, but you will need plenty of clothing layers – and don't forget extra socks to keep your feet dry.

CHILDREN AND PETS

This is an excellent walk for children, as most stages are not very strenuous. You will know your child best, and will be able to gauge their abilities. Some things to note, however: there is a lack of toilets in many areas. Also, some of the roadways can be dangerous for small children. Keep a close eye on them, especially when walking up to a road crossing, which may not be visible. Dogs are allowed on this route, although be careful in areas with traffic and livestock. Beware: if a dog worries, or chases livestock in Scotland, there can be heavy fines for the owner and the dog can be seized or even killed. Don't take your dog into a field that has lambs or calves, which can be born any time of year, but generally March–May. Also, don't allow your dog to chase birds, especially during nesting season. Pick up and remove all dog waste.

Beware of livestock coming into Clatto Den, as well as many other places on the Way. Be sure to keep dogs under control (Stage 5)

ON THE TRAIL

An official Fife Pilgrim Way 'Gateway Panel' marks the start of the Way in Culross (Stage 1)

USING THIS GUIDE

Each chapter outlines one Stage and includes a short overview of the route. You will likely have to do some planning regarding transportation and accommodation to make sure you are prepared with places to stay. We recommend starting with the Stage facilities planner at the start of this guide, which provides an overview of each stage and the amenities along the route.

At the beginning of each chapter, you will find an information box with the distance and approximate time it will take to complete the stage. While ample time has been given in these estimations, you might find that you'd like to add on some extra time for meandering, birdwatching, and picnicking. Information about accommodation, food, and other amenities is also located at the beginning of each stage.

If you are walking straight through, you will also need to choose between the two alternative starting stages. There are alternative itineraries provided for people who might want to walk the route at a faster pace. If you take this option, some of these days will be long, but they avoid some terminuses without accommodation, and if you are walking in summer, you will have plenty of daylight for a long walk. You will find an accommodation planning table in Appendix A, along with websites and phone numbers for accommodation.

WALKING THE FIFE PILGRIM WAY

The entire route is mapped out on the Ordnance Survey® 1:50,000 map excerpts included in this guide, though having a full map (as detailed in maps, below), is recommended to give you wider context and help with finding accommodation and facilities off-route. Distances, route directions, and wayfinding hints are given throughout the text, along with historical and contemporary points of interest. Appendix B and C also contain contact information and websites for sites of interest along the route.

FINDING YOUR WAY

Waymarking and access
The FPW is an easy path to follow. It is thoroughly waymarked with the FPW symbol, which is modelled from a pilgrim badge from the Middle Ages. Pilgrim badges were popular souvenirs for pilgrims walking the Way, and a collection of them can be found at the St Andrews Museum, found in the grounds of Kinburn Park. Not only is the FPW marked with waymarkers, many stages of the way are also marked by a series of 'gateways', or large information kiosks with route information and artistic maps. It is important to note that these do not necessarily correspond to the stages in this guide, but they provide helpful reference points for those walking the route, or curious passers-by. There is also a FPW 'passport' available through the FCCT. It includes spaces

The Fife Pilgrim Way is marked with both waymarker plaques and stickers

to record the date that you pass each site on the route.

Maps
Maps that cover the Fife Pilgrim Way Include: OS Explorer® Map 367 Dunfermline, Kirkcaldy & Glenrothes South, OS Explorer Map 370 Glenrothes North, Falkland & Lomond Hills, and OS Explorer Map 371 St Andrews & East Fife. There is also a Footprint Map of the entire Fife Pilgrim Way, available from Cordee Press and at local bookshops near the Way.

CHALLENGES

Physical
Know your own limits and take care of yourself. Although most of this route is fairly close to civilisation, some stages do take you through some remote countryside where help may be far off. You may not see many other people on some stretches, so be prepared in case of an emergency. Scotland is a very safe country, with low levels of violent crime. It is safe for people to walk alone, but tell someone where you are going and when you will return, just in case. You will be passing through some larger towns/cities, so keep your senses about you as you would in any urban area.

Healthcare
Scotland has excellent healthcare and medical facilities. Any of the larger towns will have pharmacies and medical clinics, with hospitals located in Dunfermline and Glenrothes, and a community hospital in St Andrews. The closest Accident and Emergency hospital is in Kirkcaldy, about 10km off the route. You can contact National Health Scotland Fife at https://www.nhsfife.org for more information. In an emergency call 999, or dial 111 for non-emergency help.

Ticks
Lyme disease is a bacterial infection transmitted by ticks, and the disease does occur in Fife. Ticks can be picked up by brushing through vegetation. Wearing long sleeves and tucking trousers into socks can help, along with insect repellent. After a day of walking, take a look at folds in your skin and if you do find a tick, remove it with tweezers or seek medical advice. Ticks are small, and can be unnoticed. If you see a red circular rash anywhere on your body, this can be a sign of Lyme disease and medical help should be sought. Roughly 30 known cases are reported in Fife each year.

Livestock
Scotland has no wild animals that cause harm to humans, but livestock can. Be aware when you are entering an area with free-ranging livestock, especially during calving or lambing season. Most cattle won't bother you, and will move aside with a loud noise, but if you see a bull in a field be aware that it can charge, and people have been seriously injured. If you have a dog and cattle charge you, keep calm, let the dog go and get out of the field. Likewise, most sheep are afraid of humans, but an angry ram could charge. If in doubt, give livestock a wide berth and know where the closest escape route is.

Fires
If the weather has been dry, take great care with fire. There have been cases of moorland fires being started accidentally. If there is exceptional fire risk, areas may be closed.

ABOUT FIFE

The garden behind the Friary Hospitium is a pleasant spot to take a rest in Inverkeithing (Stage 1A)

A BRIEF HISTORY

Fife is called a 'kingdom' because it was the home of the Scottish monarchs from King Malcolm III, who ruled between 1058 to 1093. However, there is some evidence that it may previously have been the seat of Pictish kings. As the peninsula between the Firth of Forth and the Firth of Tay, the Kingdom of Fife is ringed by coast on three sides. Fife is now a council area of Scotland. Although Fife has a population of over 350,000, it has no large cities. The Kingdom of Fife is rich in history and culture, and the people of Fife, or 'Fifers', have long been proud of their unique, and ever-diversifying kingdom.

Coal mining

Both the history and landscape of Fife have been shaped by coal mining. Monks first started mining coal in Culross in the 13th century, and the last mine was closed in 2002. Between these dates span at least 800 years of people digging coal from the earth, moving and changing the landscape forever, and fuelling an industrial society.

By as early as 1650, it is estimated that there were more than 50 large pits in fife, producing over 15,000 tonnes per year for use locally and abroad in Scandinavia and the Netherlands. With the introduction of the steam engine, mining expanded.

The Fife Coal Company was established in 1887, and produced around 50% of Fife's coal output. The industry was nationalised in 1947. At its peak around 1913, Fife collieries employed around 30,000 people. By the 1960s that number had dropped to around 19,000, still a significant industry.

The culture of Fife, too, has been shaped by coal mining. The Fife Mining School was a premier technical school for training miners from 1889 to 1972. Mining was especially dangerous, and many disasters occurred, even up until recently. In 1967, nine men lost their lives at Michael Colliery. These dangers led to a strong union culture and community, with many worker-led struggles for reforms to safety and security.

God! how I've wearied for the Spring,
To hear the birds above me sing;
And see the blue within the sky,
For there were times I thought I'd die.

Eight hours' darkness in the pit,
Dark when we got out of it,
Darkness, darkness all the while,
Not even the sunlight of a smile.

Hunger, misery, strife and pain,
Hoping, knowing hopes were in vain,
Striving snarling, trusting to
The brute in us to see us through.

God! how I've wearied for the Spring.

Poem by Joe Corrie (1894–1968), Fife miner and poet

Farming

The rich soils of inland Fife have been farmed for millennia. Cereal crops, vegetables, and soft fruit production are an important part of the economy, and along with the rest of the food production sector, provide several thousand jobs. Likewise dairy and beef cattle, poultry, pigs, and sheep are all raised on the rich fields. Large-scale fruit-growing dates back to 1191, when Lindores Abbey was founded, and pears, plums, and apples were grown and made into jam. Food4Fife and other local governmental and non-governmental organisations are working to ensure that food grown in Fife is sustainable, and uses regenerative agriculture to mitigate climate change and sequester carbon. Many farmers use organic practices, and a local network of producers is putting Fife's delicious produce on the map with local distribution and marketing.

Fife today

As with the rest of Scotland, Fife is changing, and is becoming more diverse both in terms of ethnicity and in terms of careers, as people move away from the industrial and farming past and towards the technology sector as remote work becomes increasingly viable and more desirable than the jobs open to generations past. Tourism is also booming, with Scotland increasingly popular and accessible for people around the world. Fife is a prime destination for tourists to Scotland because of its history, beaches, and golf.

A faint path trails alongside crops and farmland (Stage 4)

Renewable futures

Fife remains a centre for energy expertise and production, but now as a leader in the renewable energy transition. As you walk across Fife, you will see this transformation taking place, as wind turbines replace the coal plants of the past. Technologies such as energy storage and carbon capture and storage are also being innovated here. Scotland as a whole makes a huge contribution to renewable energy, both wind and hydro, in the UK's energy mix, with one of the largest offshore wind farms being developed off the coast of Fife.

Restored landscapes

The landscapes of Fife are undergoing a transformation on an even greater scale, as the ecosystems degraded by industrial use are restored. You will pass through some of these restored areas, including the reclaimed ash lagoons at Valleyfield, once waste from Longannet Power Station. They are now the Torry Bay Nature Reserve and have been designated a Site of Special Scientific Interest (SSSI) because of their rare plants and animals. Similarly, Lochore Meadows Country Park was the former site of the Mary Pit, and was an early and successful large-scale reclamation of a former coal mine. Between 1967 and 1976, over 1 million trees were planted, and the park that exists today is a hub of wildlife and recreational activity.

NATURAL HISTORY

Geology

Fife is divided geologically into two regions: northern Fife is Devonian (359 to 419 million years ago), primarily sedimentary and volcanic, and southern Fife is Carboniferous (299 to 359 million years ago), made up of sedimentary rocks and the coal-bearing geology that has made Fife one of the richest coal-mining areas in Britain. These coal deposits accumulated when Fife was located close to the equator, and lush tropical forests created the carbon deposits that eventually became the Fife Coalfield.

The Devonian sedimentary rocks in Fife are often red sandstone, and many fossil remains of plants and animals have been found in them. Similarly, the Carboniferous sedimentary rocks, especially limestone along the coast, are known globally for their fossilised fish and plants from this era. The Lomond Hills of Fife, including Benarty Hill along the FPW, were created by volcanic intrusions around 307 million years ago, and formed the igneous rock quartz-dolerite. Vertical 'cooling joints', where molten magma cooled, can be seen in some of the summits. Glaciers covered most of Fife during the Quaternary period, and created many of the landforms seen today, as large rocks, sand and gravel were deposited and moved across the landscape from west to east. The islands of Loch Leven were created during this time by deposits of sand.

Habitats

Fife is a region gifted with rich soils, so much of the countryside has been shaped by age-old agricultural practices, which, until recently, have not been as intensive as in many areas. Although more intensive agricultural cropping practices are now used within some fields, most of the agricultural system of Fife still maintains a rich mosaic of crops with hedgerows and woodlands, making it an ideal habitat for wildlife. Upland areas also include some important heath and grassland, and lower drainages both inland and in estuaries hold some rare bog ecosystems.

In addition to some historical plantation forests, Fife is also fortunate to have some remnant ancient woodlands, including native forests that have been intact since at least 1750, when the earliest maps included them. They contain important remnants of the woodlands that used to span most of Scotland, and contain native species such as Scots pine, birch, alder, oak, ash, hazel, and rowan. Many of Fife's plantations have been continuously harvested for a hundred years or more, and often contain non-native conifers such as Douglas fir and spruces. Some of the lesser known and rare plant species to keep an eye out for along the Way include sea buckthorn, dropwort, meadow rue, bloody cranesbill, field gentian, and birdsfoot trefoil.

Wildlife

Walking the FPW brings you in touch with the diversity of birdlife that inhabits the varied ecosystems along the way. Keep your eyes (and your binoculars!) ready for sightings of shorebirds including redshank and curlew, which can also be found foraging in fields. Waterbirds are also abundant, including great-crested grebes, moorhens, swans, many types of ducks, black-headed gulls, and the majestic heron. Nesting fulmars can be seen on coastal cliffs in the summer. One of the treats of walking the Way in the summer is the skylark, with its seemingly endless and intricate 'skysong', hovering high above the fields. Roe deer can also frequently be seen, and don't forget to look for insects, including the blue butterfly.

The path heads through fern-laden Clatto Den (Stage 5)

THE FIFE PILGRIM WAY

Passing between rich farmland and a small burn, the path heads into Leslie (Stage 3)

At the end of the stage, Pittencrieff Park lends a picturesque leadup to Dunfermline Abbey

STAGE 1
Culross to Dunfermline

Start	Culross
Finish	Dunfermline
Time	4hr 30min
Distance	13.7km (8½ miles)
Total ascent	180m
Total descent	105m
Gradient	First half is mostly flat, second half a gentle rise into Dunfermline
Terrain	Pavement, gravel path, farm track, dirt trail
Refreshments	Culross: cafes, restaurants; Cairneyhill: shops, restaurants; Crossford: shops, cafes; Dunfermline: grocery stores, shops, outdoor shop, restaurants
Toilets	West Car Park, Culross; garden centre, Cairneyhill; Pittencrieff Park, Dunfermline
Accommodation	Culross: B&Bs, self-catering; Cairneyhill: hotel (1km off route); Crossford: hotels; Dunfermline: many hotels and B&Bs

This stage begins in Culross, one of the most well-preserved 17th-century towns in Scotland; it has been a religious centre since at least the 6th century. You will travel along the coast of the Firth of Forth, through villages with long coal mining histories. The impacts of the coal industry are keenly visible in the landscape of the first half of the walk. The path then turns inland and upwards, bringing you into the working farmlands of Fife, with a final approach to Dunfermline Abbey via a grand urban glen and parkland.

There is no doubt that the Royal Burgh of Culross is a unique and beautiful town. The 'pan-tile' red roofs, a signature of the town's architecture, were brought here as ballast in ships from the continent, coming to load up on salt or coal for the return journey. It has even been used as a television set for the hit 'Outlander' series as well as many other historical dramas, yet it is a place where real people live and work. Because it is so charming, you will want to linger, wandering the tiny cobbled streets and appreciating the human scale of a town from over 300 years ago. Before you begin your pilgrimage, you might want to spend a full day here, just exploring the town and soaking up its atmosphere, and perhaps visiting its beautiful palace.

WALKING THE FIFE PILGRIM WAY

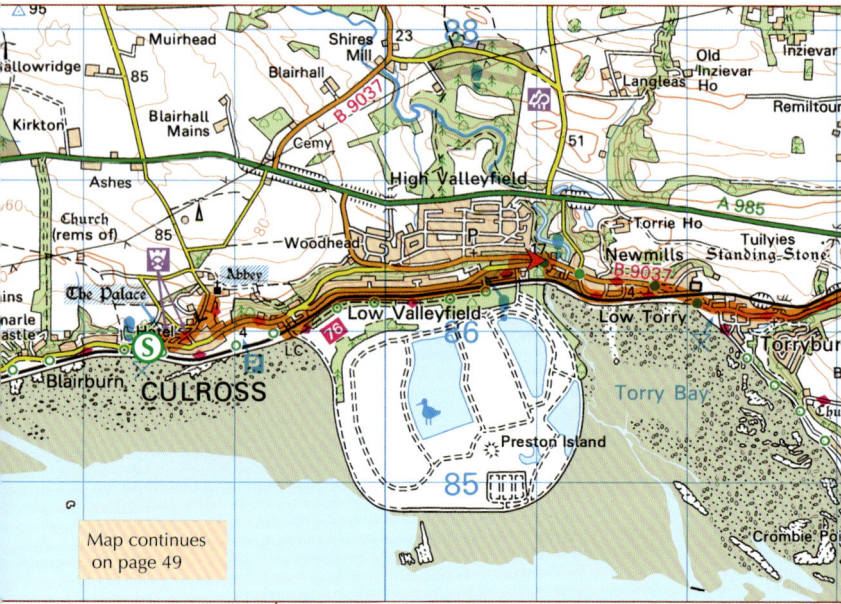

Many of the houses in **Culross** have been restored thanks to the pioneering 'Little Houses Improvement Scheme'. The programme was launched here in 1960 to prevent the demolition of many of the town's dilapidated houses. The campaign was funded by the National Trust for Scotland, and helped modernise homes while preserving their historical elements.

The official start to the FPW begins at the 'gateway' sign in the West Car Park, which has a public toilet. Follow the main road east through the town centre and the Tron and Town House, with its distinctive clock tower. ◄ Follow the cobbled Kirk Street up the hill to the left. Keep an eye out for the Lockit Well on your left, just off Erskine Brae, which is reputed to have been used by followers of Saint Serf. After 300m you will arrive at the **Abbey**, on your

Take a brief detour to see the mineshaft from Bruce's innovative coalworks under the Firth.

STAGE 1 – CULROSS TO DUNFERMLINE

right. Cistercians founded the Abbey in 1217, but it is probably built upon an earlier religious site. The church was restored in 1633, and is open to the public, as are the cemetery grounds with many interesting old graves. Inside the church, a stained-glass window from 1903 commemorates Saints Serf and Kentigern.

VISITING CULROSS PALACE

Culross Palace is managed by the National Trust for Scotland and is well worth a visit. It has a timed-entry system and tours are offered. Please note that it is only open early March to October, and the limited tickets must be purchased on the day. The Palace was the home of Sir George Bruce, who ran the town's salt-works and established an innovative coal mining operation under the Firth of Forth in the early 17th century. Some parts of the building date from 1597. The rooms are presented as they would have looked when Bruce lived there and the ambiance is palpable, especially in the dark, wood-panelled rooms. The garden is also beautiful and has been meticulously restored to be a historically accurate flower, herb, and vegetable garden from the period. There are no modern plants in the garden. There is a nice cafe (Bessie's Cafe) open year-round with highly rated cheese scones.

Visitors in Culross with the distinctive ochre coloured palace behind them

Culross has links to two important Celtic Saints: **Serf and Mungo**. Saint Serf is said to have moved here to set up a monastery after slaying a dragon, and Saint Mungo was born here after his pregnant mother washed ashore having narrowly escaped being murdered by her father. Regardless of the facts of these stories, they nonetheless established Culross as an important pilgrimage destination throughout mediaeval times.

After exploring the church, look for a marker on the ground to its front, which points you in the right direction, around the front of the church and back down the hill along a somewhat overgrown path with nettles. Don't get stung! Follow the waymarkers down to the main road, imagining you are a monk from the Abbey walking on the very same paths hundreds of years ago. Back at the main road, turn left to walk along the path. You will pass by the ruins of Saint Mungo's chapel on the left. It was built by Archbishop Blackadder in 1503 to honour Glasgow's patron saint, in what is said to be his birthplace. At the east end you can see the remains of an altar.

Look for the waymarker on your right after Pond Cottage and follow it down the footpath towards the water, crossing the train tracks. Keep immediately to the left to stay on the Fife Coastal Path for the next 3.2km as it combines with the FPW. You are now entering Torry Bay Meadows ◀ with Preston Island out to your right, which was made from coal slurry pumped from Longannet Power Station, now capped with topsoil and restored to a meadow.

Torry Bay is home to nesting birds including skylark and curlew, in addition to the rare blue butterfly.

LONGANNET POWER STATION

This area is central to the mining history of Scotland. Longannet Power Station, which dominated the skyline to the west of Culross, was once the largest coal-fired station in Europe, with a generating capacity of 2,400MW. It was the last coal-fired power station in Scotland, was decommissioned in 2016, and demolished by 2021, drawing the curtains on the industry in Scotland. Slurry from the plant created the Valleyfield Lagoons (and now Torry Bay Meadows). High Valleyfield is also the site of one of the worst mining disasters in Scotland, when 35 men were killed in an explosion.

A monument commemorating the Valleyfield Colliery reminds passersby of the rich history of coal mining in the region

Follow the gravel path for about a mile, coming to a waymarker as you take a ramp and bridge over the railway. Follow the path along the main road, which eventually becomes Main Street. You'll stroll through the small village of **Newmills** before passing under the railway bridge and into the town of **Torryburn** (**1hr 20min**), with the beach immediately to your right. There is a nice park for a picnic with views over Torry Bay.

To the south, in Torry Bay, hidden under high tides, is the resting place and grave marker of **Lilias Adie**. Lilias, a resident of Torryburn, was tortured until her confession of witchcraft. When she died in 1704, she was buried at low tide, under a slab of rock. Parts of her body were grave-robbed and held as trophies by Andrew Carnegie and St Andrews University, where her skull was located. Local residents and members of Fife Witches have commemorated her final resting place with a plaque honouring her ordeal.

The Fife Coastal Path breaks off to the right here, but continue straight and you will be on the FPW. Heading out of Torryburn, you will be walking along the pavement beside the B9037. Torry Burn itself will be trickling along to your right in a dense, ivy filled forest. Follow the waymarkers along an old paved road and carefully cross the A985 to Muirside Lane. You will cross over the railway on a bridge, and in 200m you will find the A994 and take a right into the peaceful village of **Cairneyhill** (**1hr 20min**), where there are a few shops to get supplies, as well as a cafe and toilets at the garden centre.

Keep your eye out for Cairneyhill Church where you cross over to Hilton Road to the left, which heads up into the countryside and fields of grain. Walk past the old farmhouses with a peaceful old beech forest on your right – there is an alternate, unmaintained, path through the forest. Follow the single track down the hill which becomes forested, before crossing a road on the outskirts of **Crossford** (**50min**). Head up Kirkwood Crescent, straight on until you come to a waymarker and sign pointing to Knockhouse Farm to your left and up the single-track road towards the farm in the distance. This is a working farm so be respectful and follow any signage. Make your way around and past the farm and carry on to your right following the single-track gravel road on the upper side of the barn. The track eventually turns to a grassy path between two

STAGE 1 – CULROSS TO DUNFERMLINE

fields as you head straight towards the Abbey, which you can now see in the distance. You can also glimpse the Forth bridges across the fields on your right.

At the end of the grassy path, cross the busy road to Cameron Street and walk up the residential street. At the end of the road turn right and head into **Pittencrieff Park**, where you can follow the waymarkers on a beautiful approach to the Abbey, your destination in **Dunfermline** (**1hr**). ▶

Pittencrieff Park, or 'The Glen' was given to the people of Dunfermline by Andrew Carnegie in 1902.

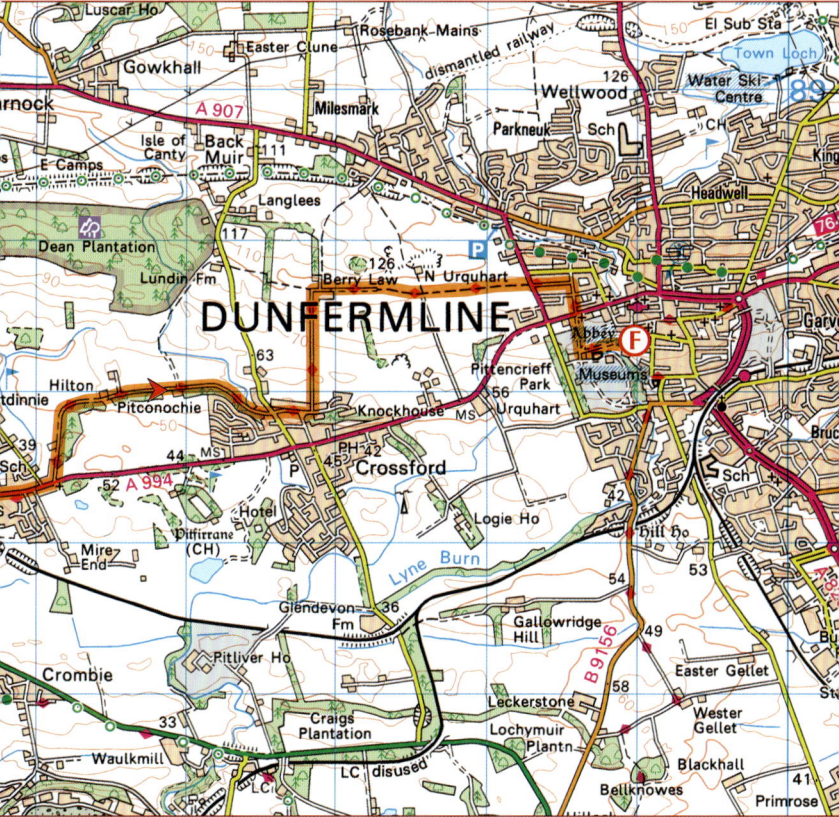

Holding a critically important place in Scottish history, **Dunfermline** was home to Scottish monarchs from 1065, leading to Fife's official name: 'the Kingdom of Fife'. In addition to its mediaeval history, Dunfermline was also the birthplace of Andrew Carnegie, the steel magnate and philanthropist, and his humble cottage is now a museum and memorial to his work across the world.

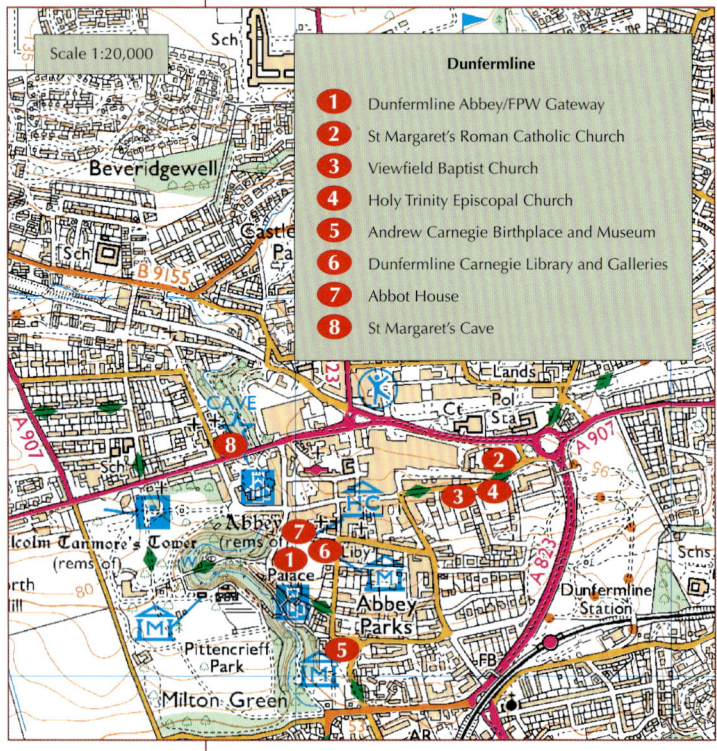

Dunfermline

1. Dunfermline Abbey/FPW Gateway
2. St Margaret's Roman Catholic Church
3. Viewfield Baptist Church
4. Holy Trinity Episcopal Church
5. Andrew Carnegie Birthplace and Museum
6. Dunfermline Carnegie Library and Galleries
7. Abbot House
8. St Margaret's Cave

Scale 1:20,000

STAGE 1A
North Queensferry to Dunfermline

Start	North Queensferry
Finish	Dunfermline
Time	4hr 30min
Distance	13.7 km (8½ miles)
Total ascent	210m
Total descent	130m
Gradient	A climb out of North Queensferry, steep at times, then fairly flat with a gentle undulating grade to Dunfermline.
Terrain	Mostly pavement and hard surfaces, but also some grassy paths
Refreshments	North Queensferry: shops, cafes and a Michelin star restaurant; shops and cafes in Inverkeithing, Rosyth and Dunfermline. Outdoor shop in Dunfermline.
Toilets	North Queensferry car park, Inverkeithing Civic Centre, Pittencrieff Park Dunfermline
Accommodation	Hostel accommodation in Edinburgh; North Queensferry: hotel and self-catering; Rosyth: hotels and B&B; Dunfermline: hotels and B&B

This route is an alternative starting stage for the Fife Pilgrim Way. Beginning in North Queensferry beneath the spectacular Forth Rail Bridge, this is where most early pilgrims would have landed after crossing the Firth of Forth to begin their journey onwards. This stage provides a kind of 'sampler', where you can experience some of the many different shades of Fife. The route takes you from the coastal cliffs of the Forth, through industrial landscapes, historic battlefields, farmlands, and housing estates, ending with a beautiful approach to Dunfermline Abbey, your final destination.

One of the two official starting points of the Fife Pilgrim Way begins at the gateway located under the Forth Rail Bridge in North Queensferry. From this vantage point at the foundation of the famous bridge, you have a stunning view of the massive engineering marvel. It is worth waiting a while to take in the small and pleasant beach and watch the trains passing overhead. ▶

You may see the red shank, also known as 'Sentinel of the Beach', a bird known for its piercing alarm call.

FORTH RAIL BRIDGE

The Forth Rail Bridge is a point of pride for Scotland, and retained its title as the longest single cantilever bridge in the world until 1919, spanning a total length of 2,467m. It was the first large structure in Britain to be made from steel. The bridge was designed by Sir John Fowler and Sir Benjamin Baker, and construction began in 1882 to replace the world's first 'train ferry', built in 1850. By the time the bridge was officially opened in 1890, it had used 55,000 tonnes of steel, 6.5 million rivets, and 640,000 cubic feet of granite. Tragically, at least 73 people are known to have died during the construction. During both World Wars, the bridge served as a major line of defence. Today, it still impresses, and in 2015 the bridge was designated a UNESCO world heritage site.

The start of the FPW under the Forth Rail Bridge in North Queensferry

This part of the FPW follows the same route as the Fife Coastal Path (FCP), so keep an eye out for either waymarkers. Follow the signs to the left and then take an immediate right up through the town of North Queensferry, passing a few cafes along the way. The path climbs steeply as you walk directly under the towering stone foundations of the Forth Rail Bridge. After half a kilometre, you enter Carlingnose Point Wildlife Reserve, previously quarried in the 1800s, and now managed by

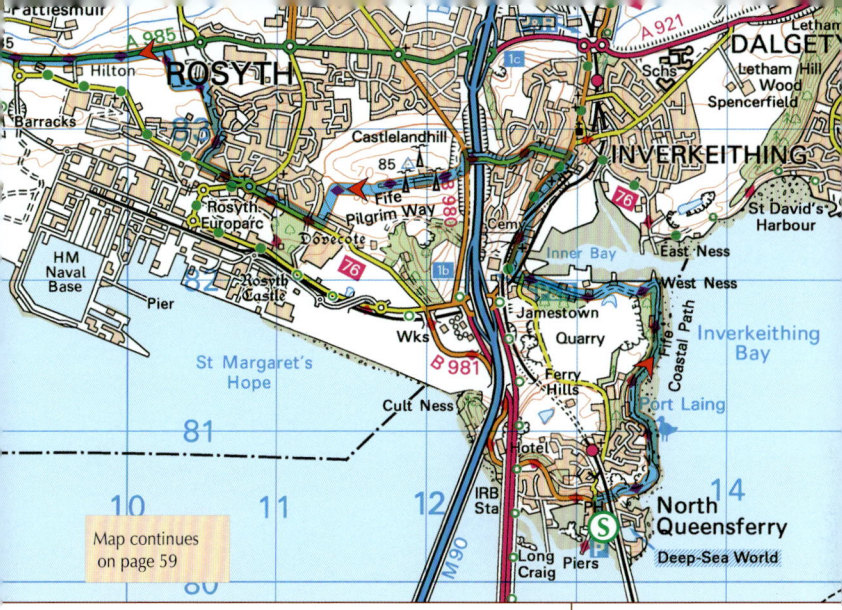

the Scottish Wildlife Trust. The area has been designated a site of special scientific interest because of its ecology.

This **landscape** boasts interesting geological features and rare plant species, including dropwort, meadow rue, bloody cranesbill, and field gentian. Birdlife includes bullfinches and warblers, as well as fulmars, which may be seen nesting in the quarry cliffs. The Cruicks Quarry was once an important source of a fine quartz dolerite called whinstone, which was in high demand, and was shipped as far away as Liverpool and London for use as material for docks, buildings, and pavements.

Follow the main path which runs along the cliff and around the quarry. ▶ The gorse and wild rose bushes open up to views across the Forth to Inchcolm Island and Bass Rock, as well as Edinburgh with its distinctive skyline sweeping from the Castle to Arthur's Seat. Eventually you arrive at a beautiful sandy strand from which to enjoy this view.

The ruined World War 1 jetty was built for landing supplies and ammunition, but is now being restored to encourage breeding terns.

The path along the water through Carlingnose Point Wildlife Reserve

As you walk along the metal scrapyard, play a game of 'I-Spy' with the items in the mountain of waste.

Rounding northwest you approach **Jamestown**, with its steel recycling and industrial works. Keep to the water at the picnic area and cross over a metal bridge into an industrial area by the pier. You will pass some high security and 'No Entry' areas as you walk past the gates of the metal yard. Keep going along a cement wall with barbed wire, don't worry: you're on the right track. ◀ Keep following the signs for the FPW/FCP. In front of you you'll see the viaduct leading towards the Forth Rail Bridge and a busier road. Turn right and follow the waymarkers, crossing the street so you can pass under the bridge. Turn right onto Hope Street as you enter the town of **Inverkeithing** (**1hr 20min**).

As you approach Inverkeithing, you will pass by a park on your right where you are reminded of some of the most shameful history in Scotland – the era of witch hunting and burning. This is **Witchknowe Park**, where at least 51 people were executed for witchcraft in the town between 1621 and 1652.

STAGE 1A – NORTH QUEENSFERRY TO DUNFERMLINE

Pass under the main railroad bridge on the B981. As well as being a good place to get some supplies or a bite to eat, Inverkeithing is home to an old Hospitium of the Greyfriars. The Hospitium is located next to Inverkeithing Civic Centre, which also has a tea shop and public toilets.

> **Inverkeithing Friary and Gardens** is one of the best-preserved examples of an urban mediaeval friary in Scotland. The Franciscans, also called Greyfriars due to the colour of their robes, established the friary in the mid-14th century. The Franciscan Hospitium still stands today, where it used to provide lodging for pilgrims. The building is currently undergoing redevelopment and it is hoped that the Inverkeithing friary will eventually hold accommodation and a cafe for tourists and pilgrims, but for now, the friary garden makes a nice spot for a picnic with a view over the Firth of Forth.

At Inverkeithing the FPW leaves the FCP. In the centre of town look for the sign pointing left up a steep road called Hill Street. As you round the top of the hill, keep going towards the countryside, crossing the M90 on a bridge. Turn right on Castlandhill Road and take the immediate left onto a small curving road, following it to the top of the hill where you will find beautiful views of the Firth of Forth all the way across to Edinburgh with the Pentland Hills behind. ▶

From here you can see all three of the Forth bridges: the rail bridge and the two road bridges, including the newer Queensferry Crossing, which opened in 2017.

> Castlandhill is the location of the important **Battle of Inverkeithing**, which took place in 1651. It was the final battle of the Wars of the Three Kingdoms, bringing Scotland under control of Oliver Cromwell. On this hill, 4,500 Parliamentarians, including cavalry, attacked around the same number of Scottish infantry, who eventually retreated and took heavy losses. It is thought that around 760 Scottish infantrymen died that day and around 1000 were taken prisoner.

As you reach the end of the paved road, continue along a single track through the field. In the distance, you can see the flames of oil refineries and shipyard cranes of Rosyth Dockyard. Follow the grassy path alongside a hawthorn hedgerow, with the waymarkers turning left at the end of the field. The trail is faint but visible heading downhill, towards **Rosyth** (**40min**). Take a sharp right into the housing estate and at Ferry Toll Road turn right. There is a pavement for walking. Here you have joined the FCP again. Just after the roundabout cross the road and cut over to Hilton Road, which leads away from the Firth.

Cross the road and turn right up Wilson Way towards the Rosyth FC pitches, after which turn left on the public footpath. As you pass along the edge of meadow and a small woodland, you'll get a view of Dunfermline in the distance: your destination at the end of this stage. The next section of the route takes you along the A985, which is a busy road with a small pavement. Take care. After about 1000m, cross the road and head up towards Douglasbank Cemetery. ◀ Here, the Fife Coastal Path departs again, to the left, but you will be heading inland.

The Douglasbank Cemetery is a peaceful resting place, with many graves from World War 1 and 2.

The next section of the route takes you through some lovely countryside, old forest and fields. Massive old beech trees make this a special, hidden, little glen. Follow the waymarks along the winding path. Eventually you reach a gravel path. Take a right onto a small gravel road and head up

This segment approaches Dunfermline Abbey from the SE, passing first through the Pends

STAGE 1A – NORTH QUEENSFERRY TO DUNFERMLINE

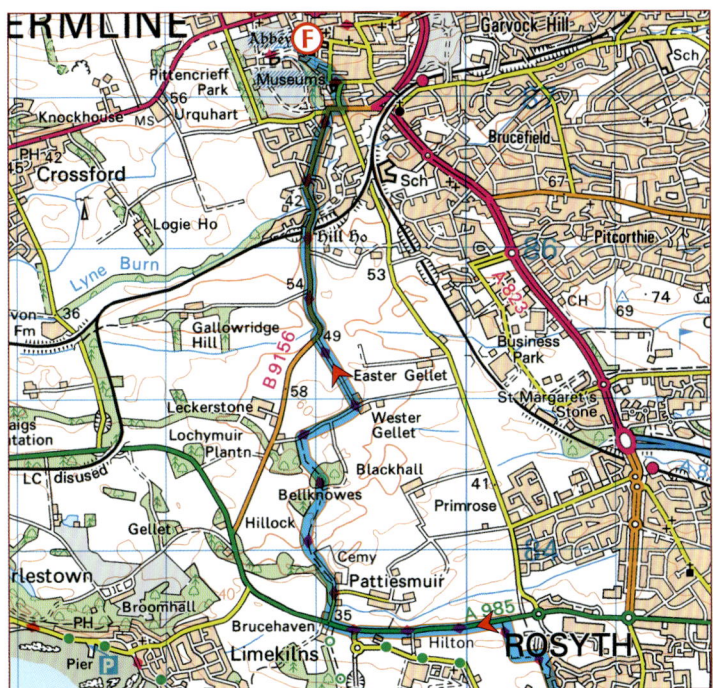

through a working farm, turning left, just before the barns. At the end of the gravel track turn right, walking along a narrow path along a busy, winding road. Be careful, especially as you cross the railway bridge, as it is quite narrow. This is one of the longer stretches of busy road you will find on the FPW. Although it is not the most peaceful and remote part of the walk, it is still quite pleasant countryside and you can see Dunfermline Abbey in the distance.

You approach **Dunfermline** (**2hr 30min**) through its quiet suburbs. Follow the waymarkers up Moodie Street, bearing left to pass Andrew Carnegie's Birthplace and Museum (on your right). Continue up St Margaret Street and you will reach the entrance of Dunfermline Abbey through a gateway on your left, the final stop on this stage. ▶

While you won't find the monks' brewhouse or bakehouse, within the abbey grounds, you will find a lovely, cosy tea shop with home-baked goods (open until 4pm most days).

DUNFERMLINE ABBEY AND PALACE

Dunfermline Abbey and the palace ruins that lie within its grounds are not to be missed. The Abbey was built between 1128 and 1150 by David I, on the site of a Culdee church. Culdees, or Céile Dé, were an early Celtic Christian monastic sect that were eventually persecuted by the state-sanctioned church. The Abbey eventually became the first Benedictine abbey in Scotland. St Margaret died in 1093, and pilgrims have since come from great distances to visit her relics and tomb, which are said to cause many healing miracles. Indeed, the nave-water in the Abbey is still considered to be healing.

In addition to once holding St Margaret's relics, many famous individuals are buried here, including Scottish kings David I and Robert the Bruce. The interior of the Abbey was destroyed during the Reformation in 1559 and 1560, along with the removal of St Margaret's relics when the monks left in 1563. The monks took her 'head shrine', which included her head and hair, to France. The relic was later either destroyed or lost in the French Revolution.

Visitors can wander throughout the nave of the abbey for free, and it is open to visitors on most days until 4pm or 5pm with tours from Historic Environment Scotland. It contains striking Romanesque architecture that is uniquely well-preserved after most examples were destroyed during the Scottish Reformation. The stained-glass windows are particularly striking and include images of Queen Margaret, William Wallace, and Robert the Bruce.

The parish church, where Robert the Bruce's tomb is located, is operated by the Church of Scotland, and was built in 1821. It is open to visitors March to late October every day. The ruins of the palace are also open to the public and cared for by Historic Environment Scotland. The palace was used by Scottish monarchs until the early 17th Century. Charles I was born here in 1600, and was the last monarch born in Scotland.

STAGE 2
Dunfermline to Kelty

Start	Dunfermline
Finish	Kelty
Time	4hr 30min
Distance	13.2km (8¼ miles)
Total ascent	210m
Total descent	170m
Gradient	Steady climb then a steep climb up to the second-highest point on the Way
Terrain	Gravel road, and road with large rocks, mix of pavement and trails
Refreshments	Dunfermline: many shops, restaurants, cafes, pubs; Kelty: small shops, restaurants, pubs
Toilets	Pittencrieff Park, Dunfermline; Kelty Community Centre, Kelty
Accommodation	Dunfermline: many hotels and B&Bs; Craigduckie Shepherd Huts (2km off route); none at terminus in Kelty, options via bus to Dunfermline, or bus/taxi to Kinross

For the first three kilometres of this stage, you will walk through the town of Dunfermline, where you can see traces of St Margaret's presence, before climbing up along a country road to the mining town of Kingseat. After Kingseat, the path becomes more varied, as you pass through a landscape altered by the coal industry, including the peaceful Loch Fitty and St Ninian's opencast mine. The stage finishes with a pleasant jaunt through a woodland into the quiet village of Kelty. Unless you are wild camping, The terminus in Kelty does not have accommodation, so you will have to plan ahead for an alternative.

From the official FPW 'gateway' in front of Dunfermline Church, head up St Catherine's Wynd and turn right on Maygate, which brings you in front of the Abbot House, or 'the Pink Hoose', as the locals call it. ▶ The street then becomes Abbot Street as you pass the Dunfermline Carnegie Library and Galleries, which feature a local history museum, art galleries, and award-winning cafe. This area is not well signposted.

Abbot House has a lovely cafe and recreated 17th-century formal garden, lovingly put together by Beechgrove Garden in 1995.

Andrew Carnegie was born in Dunfermline in 1835. Born to a weaving family, he emigrated to the US with his family at the age of 12. There he became one of the wealthiest American industrialists, most famously through Pittsburgh's Carnegie Steel Company. He eventually gave away almost 90% of his wealth, leading a philanthropic movement. The humble cottage he was born in is now the Andrew Carnegie Birthplace Museum, on Moodie Street.

Turn left onto Guildhall Street. At the top of the road you will see the Mercat Cross, where you turn right onto High Street, which has an outdoor supplies shop if you need to stock up. The road becomes East Port until you see St Margaret's Church on the left. Continue around the front of the church and follow the waymarkers to cross the busy roundabout. Head down the hill on Holyrood Place. Before the next roundabout, turn right to cross the road and walk down Leys Park Road, a paved cycle path leading out of Dunfermline. ◂

What was once Leys Park Poor House will be on your left.

Leys Park Poor House

STAGE 2 – DUNFERMLINE TO KELTY

FINDING ST MARGARET IN DUNFERMLINE

Dunfermline was, and still is, a significant place of pilgrimage for followers of St Margaret, although finding her presence here can be difficult. Here are a few clues if you would like to seek her out:

- Dunfermline Abbey held the tomb of St Margaret, and for hundreds of years was the site of pilgrimage. She brought Benedictine monks to Dunfermline, and was buried in the Church of the Holy Trinity in 1093, on the site of the Lady Chapel, which is now ruins, having been destroyed in the Reformation. Her former tombstone has been considered a place of miracles since the 12th century.
- Although St Margaret's tomb and most of her body were lost during the Reformation, a relic of St Margaret can be found at St Margaret's Memorial Roman Catholic Church. As you leave Dunfermline, the church is located along the FPW. It holds a shoulder bone that was returned to Scotland from Spain in 1863, where it was cared for by nuns in Edinburgh until 2008. The church is generally open on weekdays and there are depictions of several local saints as well as St Margaret. The Lady chapel, where her relic is located, is a small chapel to the right of the altar.
- St Margaret's Cave has become a difficult place to visit, since it was vandalised and closed. However, if you plan ahead, you can still go inside. The cave is said to be a place where she came to pray 900 years ago. Strangely, it is now located beneath a car park, and is accessed through a tunnel and eighty-seven steps, where you will find an underground cavern and a life-sized statue of the St Margaret praying. The cave entrance is located at Glen Bridge car park, Chalmers Street. The best way to find opening times, or arrange a visit, is to call 01383 602365 two weeks in advance.
- An annual St Margaret Pilgrimage is held every June, with an ecumenical service at Dunfermline Abbey, a procession to her tomb, and then to a mass at St Margaret's Memorial Church.
- Abbot House has an exhibit on St Margaret and a replica of her medieval head shrine.
- St Margaret's stone is also nearby. It is said that the saint sat and rested on the stone in 1069. It is off the FPW, located on Pitreavie Way in Dunfermline.

At the end of the cycle path, take a left and head towards the main road, B912. At the T-intersection, take a

WALKING THE FIFE PILGRIM WAY

> On the right is a memorial to those many miners who lost their lives in the mines.

right to stay on the B912, as you head into the hills and countryside. There is a nice footpath along this stretch until you reach **Kingseat** (**2hr**), with views across the hills of Fife, the Forth Bridges, and the Hill of Beath to your east. Bear left as you walk through the mining village of Kingseat. ◄

Kingseat was created as a village to house miners in the late 1800s. It was a thriving **coal mining community** until the last mine closed in 1946. Coal has had a much longer history here, however, with mining taking place here since the mid 1700s, and some records pointing to coal being dug here for the 'monks of Dunfermline Abbey'.

Shortly after you leave the village, the path ends. Take the gated road to your left.

> At the base of the loch, you will find a black 'sand' beach, which is made of coal.

The path meanders through meadows and wetlands rich with bird life, including great-crested grebes, moorhens, swans, and black headed gulls, as it leads to Loch Fitty. ◄ Follow the waymarkers as you walk past a large white stables towards St Ninian's opencast mine. Take a left through the gate and walk along an old unused road through the field.

A swan swims on the waters of Loch Fitty

WALKING THE FIFE PILGRIM WAY

As you round the top of the hill you can see St Ninian's opencast mine, with its art sculptures. The mine closed in 2013 and started to be transformed into landscape art by Charles Jencks. This was only partially completed. Keep your eyes out for birds of prey as you walk through this reclaimed area, with the scars of mining still clearly visible. This is a long climb of about 2.5km on a gravel road with large rocks underfoot. At the top of the hill, you meet the B914. This is the second-highest point on the Way. Carefully cross and walk along it about 30m to the left, until you see signage for Forestry Scotland and Blairadam. Turn right towards the parking area.

The next part of the walk leads you through a forest plantation, with newer, restored forest of mixed hardwood and older-style monocrop plantations of non-native conifers, much of which have been built over former mines. You will eventually reach a gravel track – turn right. After 400m, turn right again and follow the track towards the M90, which will pass above you. Leaving the din of the M90 behind, you cross a beautiful small burn and an idyllic valley which seems to have been lost to time, and, indeed, the wood on your right has: it is officially one of the few remaining ancient woodlands in Fife. The path brings you down into the small and peaceful village of **Kelty** (**2hr 30min**), ending this stage at the main street.

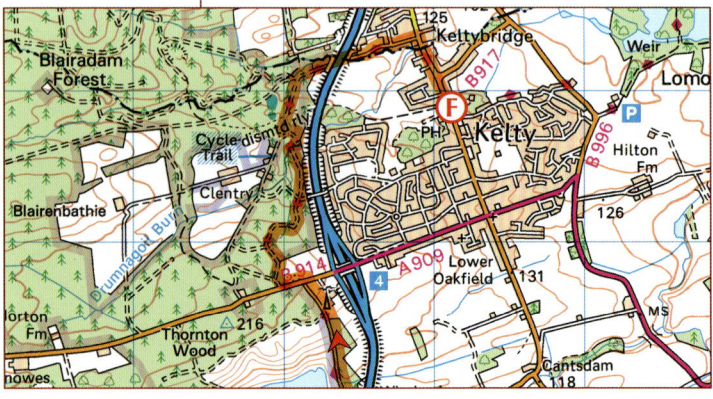

STAGE 2 – DUNFERMLINE TO KELTY

ACCOMMODATION AROUND KELTY

Unfortunately, there is no accommodation directly at the end of Stage 2 in Kelty. Hopefully, some accommodation will be developed either here in Kelty, or in the Lochore area (early in the next stage) in the near future. If you are not wild camping, some options include:
- Take a taxi or walk to nearby accommodation such as Craigduckie Shepherd Huts or Balmule House (near Loch Fittie), or the Beath Inn or Woodside Hotel in Cowdenbeath (about 4km).
- Catch a Bus back to Dunfermline and stay there for the night, returning again to Kelty to take the next stage. Bus 7D runs from Kelty to Dunfermline Bus Station.
- Another alternative is to take a 15-minute-long bus ride to Kinross, a small town on the banks of Loch Leven. Kinross has several hotels, as well as restaurants and shops.

Artwork tops the hills of St Ninian's opencast mine

WALKING THE FIFE PILGRIM WAY

STAGE 3
Kelty to Leslie

Start	Kelty
Finish	Leslie
Time	5hr 40min
Distance	16.7km (10¼ miles)
Total ascent	170m
Total descent	175m
Gradient	Very gradual downhill with a steep, short climb coming out of Kinglassie
Terrain	Gravel paths, pavement and grass trails
Refreshments	Kelty: small shops, restaurants, pubs; Lochore Meadows County Park Cafe; Crosshill: small shop; Kinglassie: pubs, small shops; Leslie: shops and cafes;
Toilets	Kelty Community Centre, Kelty; Lochore Meadows
Accommodation	Leslie: B&B

This stage is a little longer than the previous stages, and picks up in the village of Kelty, with an easy 4km walk through a beautiful stretch traversing Lochore Meadows Country Park. After passing through the village of Crosshill, the path climbs up a hill for a kilometre as you cross another stretch of countryside walking for another 2.5km, on a quiet lane through farmland and forest. The walk then follows some B-roads, again relatively flat, but along some narrow pavement for about three kilometres. After coming to the village of Kinglassie, there is a short, 2km climb over a hill, passing Finglassin's Well, a sacred spot for pilgrims. The final 2km of the stage follow the River Leven through a wooded glen into the town of Leslie, a suburb of Glenrothes.

The name 'Kelty' is derived from the Gaelic word Coiltean or 'Woodlands' and the area has been managed as a woodland since at least the 16th century.

Leave Kelty by walking to the North East along White Gates Terrace, in the centre of the village. ◄ The small cul-de-sac becomes a walking path between two tall fences, leading into the countryside. Off to your left are lovely views of Benarty Hills and Woods. The path ends at the B996, a busy road. Turn right and walk along the pavement, crossing over to the left as the road turns.

Stage 3 – Kelty to Leslie

There is a clear sign for **Lochore Meadows Country Park** (**30min**). The park was once an industrial landscape, and the site of the Mary Colliery, but its 1200 acres have been restored and reclaimed to become a cherished outdoor recreation site, referred to as 'the Meedies' by locals. ▸

As you pass through the gate, you'll be walking on an easy gravel path through the park. Keep an eye out for the FPW markers, as there are multiple, meandering paths that could easily lead you astray. You'll be keeping to the north side of the Loch, although there is an alternative path to the south, it is not the official FPW.

There are bird hides throughout the park, so if you have some extra time, you may want to take a moment to look for herons, ducks, and other birdlife. The path becomes paved as you walk through a peaceful re-planted native forest with mixed Scots Pine and hardwoods. About 500m after the path becomes paved, take a left heading towards the car park (there is no waymarker here). The path follows the edge of the loch, opening up to lovely views across the countryside with wind turbines in the distance.

There are many benches for picnic spots along the loch, or continue on the Lochside Cafe which serves hot food and drinks. The building also hosts a FPW gateway

In mediaeval times, most pilgrims would have made their way north from Kelty to Loch Leven and Scotlandwell, but the FPW takes a more southerly route.

The way out of Kelty is flanked by rose bushes

WALKING THE FIFE PILGRIM WAY

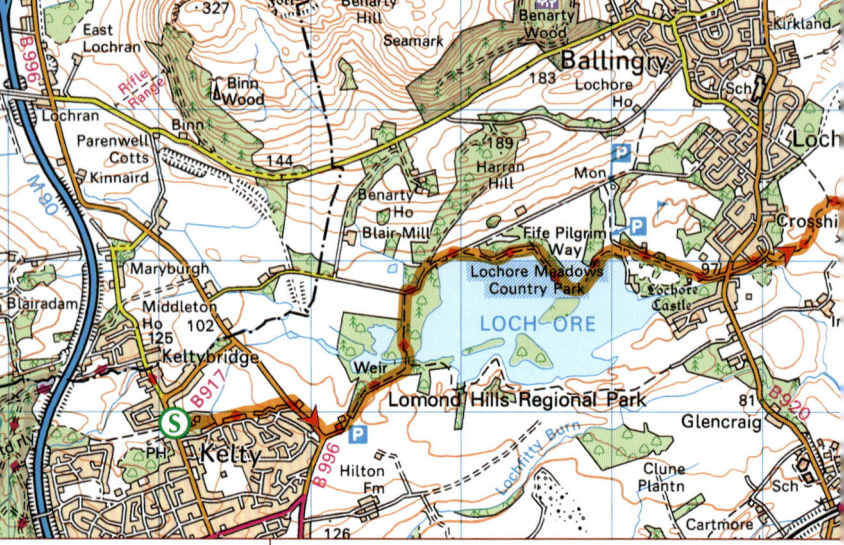

and displays some history of the area. To the north of the cafe and mining-themed playpark, Mary Pit minehead, which closed in 1966, is one of only two still standing in Fife, and serves as a memorial to the industry that was so important to this region.

Continue on the FPW from the front of the cafe towards Crosshill. The ruins of **Lochore Castle** are to your right.

> **Lochore Castle**, now ruined, was built in the 14th century as a defensive tower house, originally surrounded by the Loch. The island on which it was built was called *Inchgall* or *Innis Gall* meaning 'island of non-Gaels' in Gaelic, a possible reference to the castle's French occupants. Earlier still, it is possible that the island was once the site of an Iron Age, above-water settlement, or crannog. Loch Ore was drained in 1790 and gradually refilled in the mid-20th century.

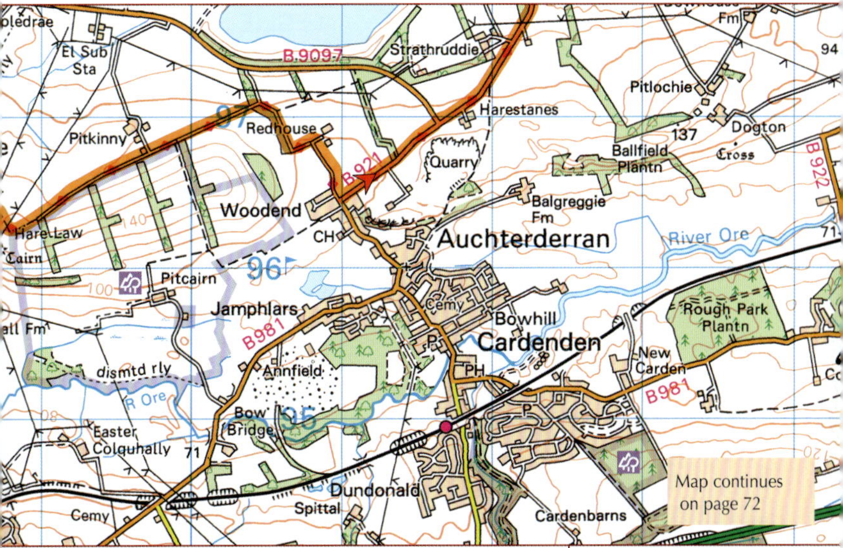

Stage 3 – Kelty to Leslie

Map continues on page 72

The Mary Pit minehead, while no longer in use, still stands sentinel

WALKING THE FIFE PILGRIM WAY

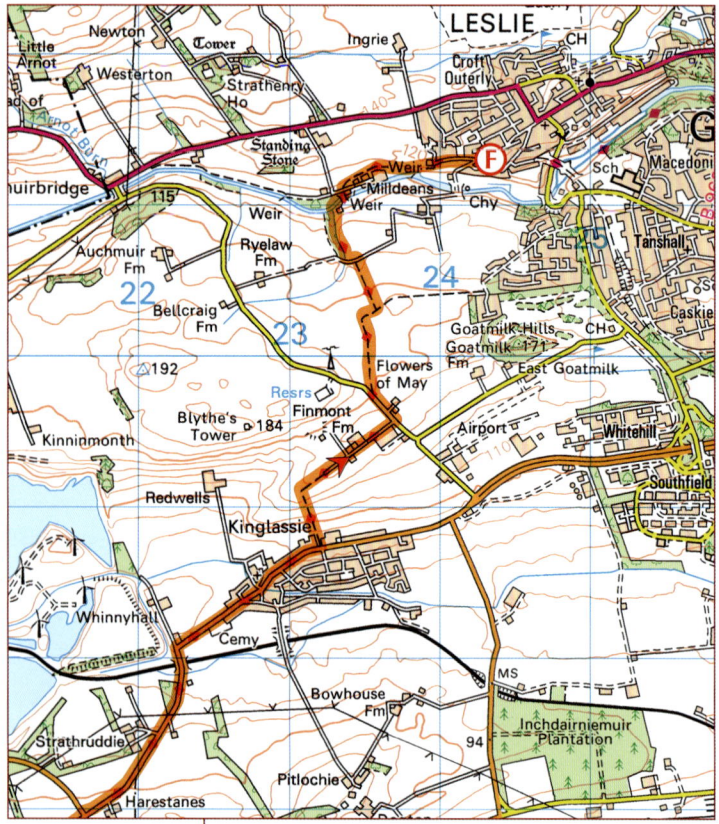

   When you enter **Crosshill** (**50min**), cross the road and head down Park Street to the left of the roundabout. Follow the waymakers and cut up to a grassy trail on your right before the end of the road – it is easy to miss. The path cuts between some pleasant hedgerows and rises gently coming out of Crosshill, about 1km, to reach **Hare Law Cairn**, about 100m off to your right after the powerlines, which was a Bronze Age burial site, but was destroyed by Victorian excavations. Follow the straight track, with easy walking for about 2km, passing farms and plantation trees. The hill to your right is a man-made pile of mining spoils from Westfield mine. This track is called 'Torres Loan', which means Torry's Cattle Track. Turning right at the fork, you can see the village of **Woodend** in the distance. Follow the track and the waymarkers through some gates, eventually reaching a new housing development and a FPW sign with a map leading to the nearby Cardenden train station (about 0.8km off the FPW). ▶ Head left on the B921, for a 3km section of narrow pavement-walking along a busy road. Be especially careful walking downhill into Kinglassie as cars will be coming behind you.

The village church in Auchterderran is about 500m to the south, and there is a reference to it from 1059, which associates it strongly with St Serf's monastery on Loch Leven and the Culdees.

The wind turbines of **Fife Environmental Energy Park Westfield** can be seen to the north. The site was once one of the UK's largest opencast coal mines, but is now an energy recovery facility, which burns landfill waste to generate electricity.

After crossing an abandoned railway line, follow the main road to the right towards the village of **Kinglassie**

Sheep keeping an eye on who is passing by

(**2hr 50min**). There is a FPW gateway here. Carry on through the town past the Miners Welfare Institute Bowling Green and look for a long rock wall and gateway on your left. Follow the grassy path leading up the hill and out of the village. Finglassen's well is about 360m off the FPW, but is worth a detour: as you head uphill out of town, a signpost points west on a small grassy path. ◀

> Finglassen's Well may have been used by pilgrims on their way to St Andrews, and it has been lovingly restored.

There is some debate about the name **Kinglassie**. Some think it derives from the Gaelic word *Cill* for monk's cell or church, and a saint's name, possibly St Glaisine from Ireland. Alternatively, it could be derived from the Gaelic word *glais*, meaning burn, hence *Fionn-glais*, or 'white, pure, holy burn' was turned into Finglassin's Well. We may never know the real meaning, but it is a holy well either way!

Return to the grassy path and head up the hill on a short, but very steep ascent. ◀ Passing through the gate, take a right along the side of a field. You will be greeted with beautiful views of the Fife countryside, and the entrance to the Firth of Forth in the distance. Continue past the farm buildings and keep in mind that this is a working farm. Coming to a T junction, cross to the road and head left for 200m until you reach a public path to Leslie and Glenrothes. The path becomes a narrow track through tall grass, as you head back into the countryside and beautiful rich farmland. A burn rolls down the hills along with you to meet the River Leven, crossing it and entering the outskirts of Glenrothes in the village of **Leslie** (**1hr 30min**), which was an important papermill town. You can still see the remains of the mills along the river.

> As you round the crest of the hill you'll see Blythe's Tower to the north, a folly built in 1812, but used as a lookout during World War 2.

The path skirts along the southern edge of Leslie, cutting through a neighbourhood on both roads and footpaths. There are limited waymarkers here though, so be sure to pay attention. While on Prinlaws Road keep an eye for the path on the right, pass through the car barrier to head towards Valley Drive which you will turn left on. Take the next right on to Valley Gardens which you will follow to then end where you will pick up at trail to Glenrothes.

STAGE 4
Leslie to Kennoway

Start	Leslie
Finish	Kennoway
Time	5hr 15min
Distance	16km (10 miles)
Total ascent	100m
Total descent	150m
Gradient	Brief uphill climb out of Glenrothes, then a gentle downhill grade all the way to Kennoway
Terrain	A mix of pavement, fine gravel and grass
Refreshments	Leslie: shops and cafes; Glenrothes: many shops and restaurants; Markinch: shops and cafes; Windygates: pub, shops; Kennoway: pub, grocery and restaurant
Toilets	Markinch Station
Accommodation	Leslie: B&B; Glenrothes: hotels; Balfarg/Gilvenbank: FPW passes Gilvenbank Hotel; Balbirnie: Balbirnie House Hotel also on FPW; Markinch: hotels; none in Kennoway but Leven (5km off route/10min taxi or 15min bus journey) has hotel, guesthouses and B&Bs

This stage makes for an easy day of walking, first through the 'New Town' of Glenrothes along a wooded path alongside the River Leven. The only uphill portion of this stage is a brief one as you leave Glenrothes through a suburban landscape which still hides some prominent neolithic sites, including two stone circles. The next 10km are all a gentle downhill walk through quintessential Fife countryside and villages into the small town of Kennoway.

Continuing in Leslie, on the outskirts of Glenrothes, turn right on Valley Gardens, entering a small residential neighbourhood.

> Glenrothes is one of Scotland's five **New Towns**. New Towns were planned towns created as a way to provide housing for what were seen as 'over-populated' inner cities (especially Glasgow) after

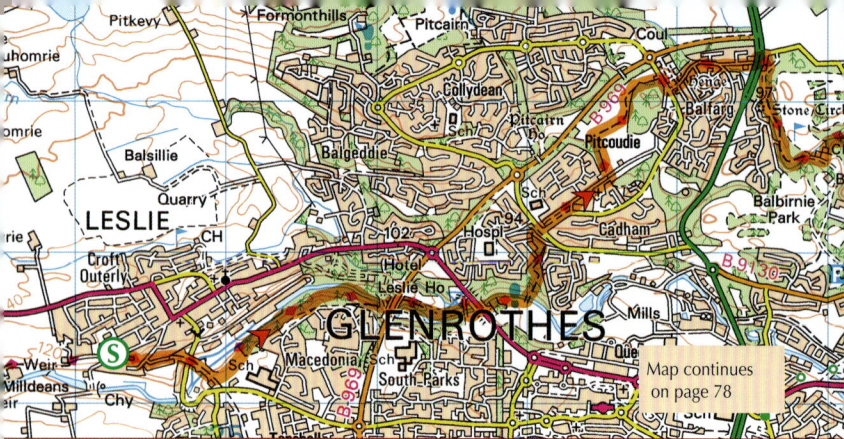

Look for the old Mill Pond and working paper mills off to your left, a sign of the river's ongoing importance for the economy.

World War 2. They were an experiment in modern town planning, and re-housed tens of thousands of people. Architects and planners were tasked with building modern homes with tight budgets and short timelines, and some say that the utopian ideals were not realised in the somewhat repetitive architecture. You may disagree, depending on your perspective on modernist and brutalist architecture.

Continue straight on the walking path over the Leslie Railway Viaduct, an impressive, 25m-high structure. ◀ After the bridge, take a left and follow the path into the forest and along the River Leven for the next 3km.

The **River Leven** flows from Loch Leven to the Firth of Forth, and it has been an important source of water and power for mills, including linen weaving, iron works, and paper mills. Impacts from these industries have degraded the river, but it is now being restored for fish, wildlife, and people. Part of this restoration involves the removal of two blockages: Burn Mill and Kirkland Dams, allowing fish-passage. Large tree trunks have also been placed along the banks to provide habitat, and native trees and wetland plants are being planted. This is an ongoing project, and you may see signs of the restoration work taking place.

Pilgrims head through a quiet forest in Glenrothes

WALKING THE FIFE PILGRIM WAY

The path roughly follows the south side of the river, although there is a brief zig-zag across to the north side after you meet the B969, which crosses above you on a suspension bridge. Keep your eyes out for FPW waymarkers, as there are many serpentine pathways through Riverside Park. Cross back to the south side of the river right before you walk under the A911. This area has many picnic tables. ◀ Cross the river again at the play park, and head to the north, leaving the river behind. Follow the waymarkers up the paved footpaths into a quiet neighbourhood. After an underpass, continue straight ahead on a residential street. The FPW takes you around the Glenrothes Community sports fields and into Gilvenbank Park. When you meet Huntsman's Road, take a right and an immediate left onto Kilmichael Road, which curves around. Take any of the roads to your right and head into the centre of the development to find **Balfarg Henge** (**2hr**).

Balfarg Henge is one of the only large Neolithic ceremonial sites in Eastern Scotland, dating from around 3200BC. Built by some of the first farmers

> Riverside Park also contains a labyrinth you can walk, a tradition associated with pilgrimage. It is located between the wildlife pond and the skate park.

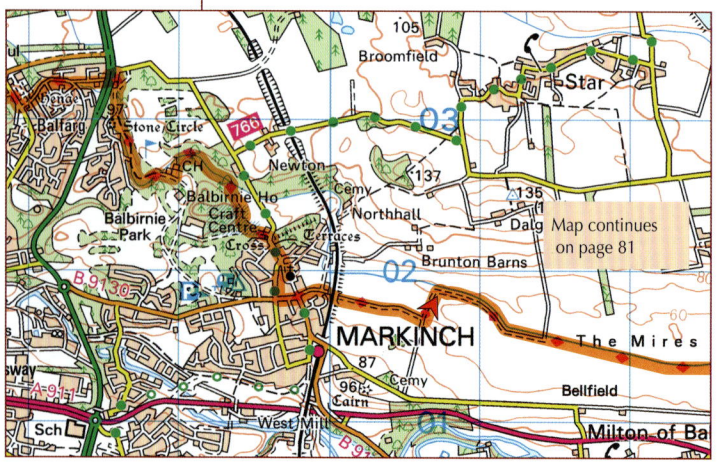

Balbirnie Stone Circle

in the region, it was in use for hundreds of years. The henge was built in two phases, first a ditch and bank with wooden posts in six concentric circles. Around 2800BC, megaliths replaced the posts, and it later became a burial site. Only two stones remain, but its situation at the centre of the modern development lends a sense of ongoing reverence nonetheless.

After a stop at the henge, head back to the route on Kilmichael Road and take Balfarg Steadings towards the A892, which you will cross. Take a sharp right and tuck into the woods on a small trail until you meet Tofthill Road. Continue walking 200m and follow the red gravel path on your left. **Balbirnie Stone Circle** is nestled behind a berm immediately to your right.

Balbirnie Stone Circle is a reconstructed stone circle with eight stones of the original ten. It was last used around 3000BC, when it contained four stone cists for burials and/or cremation. There is a cup-marked stone, whose meaning is lost to time.

Look for the Stob Cross, a Pictish stone with a cross on one side and a battle scene on the other.

Keep your eyes out for the waymarkers through **Balbirnie Park**, as there are several unmarked paths. Stick to the left passing in front of the Balbirnie Golf Club. Continue on the path for 100m before crossing the burn, walking alongside it for the next few minutes before crossing back over the burn and turning right. Stay on this path as it winds its way out of the park. The park is filled with many varieties of old rhododendrons and a beautiful glade full of botanical wonders. After the park, you will meet Stob Cross Road. Take a right, heading down into the well-preserved village of **Markinch** (**45min**), where there is a FPW gateway. ◀

Pass under the rail bridge and head away from Markinch and back into the countryside

STAGE 4 – LESLIE TO KENNOWAY

The tower of **St Drostan's church** dates from around 1200, and is the site of an early Celtic religious community, possibly the Culdees, from the 6th century. The current parish church itself has seen many modifications, but the manse next door, Mansefield, retains some walls from the 13th century, and was used as a place for pilgrims to rest on their journey from Dunfermline and St Andrews.

Exit Markinch by walking down Commercial Street then left on Brunton Road, and under the railway. The next 3km of the trail is a stretch through what is known as 'The Mires'. While this sounds ominous, it is actually a nice walk through open countryside. Look for wildlife including skylarks and deer. ▶ You will start to see the village of **Windygates** ahead of you, including the Cameronbridge Distillery in the distance.

Follow the waymarker, taking a left on Fa-Latch Road, a single-track lane behind houses. After about 600m you will reach the A916. Take a left and follow the pavement up the hill into the town of **Kennoway** (**2hr 30min**), where this stage ends.

The Mires were once a marshland and an area for gathering reeds for thatch and peat for fuel. The trail you are walking is the Braes Loan, once an ancient cattle track.

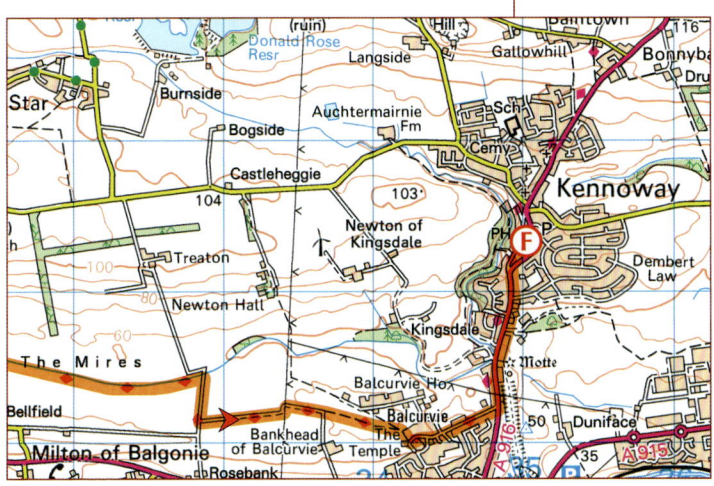

STAGE 5
Kennoway to Ceres

Start	Kennoway
Finish	Ceres
Time	4hr 45min
Distance	14km (8¾ miles)
Total ascent	240m
Total descent	235m
Gradient	The most challenging stage in terms of gradient, you will be steadily climbing Clatto Hill, the highest point on the journey, before descending for the second half of the stage
Terrain	Mainly gravel roads, farm tracks and paths along fields, but also some pavements
Refreshments	Kennoway: pub, shop and restaurants; Ceres: cafes, small shops, pubs
Toilets	Public toilets in Ceres
Accommodation	None in Kennoway, but hotel, guesthouses, B&Bs in Leven (5km via 10min taxi or 15min bus journey from Kennoway); Ceres: Hotel, B&Bs

This stage brings you deeper into the Fife countryside, climbing through working farm- and forest-land to the highest point on the FPW: Clatto Hill (248m). The path then steadily descends for the rest of the stage, passing through the peaceful Clatto Den. Next, a long, straight stretch on the Waterless Way draws you through an ancient track crossing fields of grain and produce, displaying the rich farmlands of Fife. These are fields that have been worked for centuries and paths that have been walked the same. The stage ends in the historic market town of Ceres with the Fife Folk Museum and Bishop's Bridge.

From the town centre of Kennoway, take the next street to the west and meet up with The Causeway, the original road through town, lined with former weavers' cottages and other historic buildings. Continue past the cemetery

STAGE 5 – KENNOWAY TO CERES

through the old town and you will meet the A916, the main road out of town, heading north. ▶

Kennoway Parish Church was dedicated to **St Kenneth** in the late 12th century. St Kenneth, or Cainneach of Aghaboe, was a mediaeval Irish missionary who lived from about AD515–600, and was a friend of St Columba. The Kennoway Den, along the burn to the west of the village, has a cave that was said to be where St Kenneth lived and prayed. Because of this, The Causeway is still referred to as St Kenneth's Causeway.

Follow the road out of town for about 300m and carefully cross after you pass the sign for Bonnybank. Head up the lane between the sign and the houses, which eventually becomes a path between hedgerows and houses. Cross the single-track road and continue walking on a farm track for about 1km, passing working dairy farms and lots of birdlife. Looking back, you get sweeping views across the Firth of Forth, where you began your journey.

When you reach a large barn, pass around the gate and continue on an overgrown farm track. Eventually a

You pass St Kenneth's Parish Church, which has the oldest communion cups still in use in Scotland, one dating from 1671.

Be careful passing through Ovenstone Plantation, an active logging area, as there may be machinery or missing waymarkers

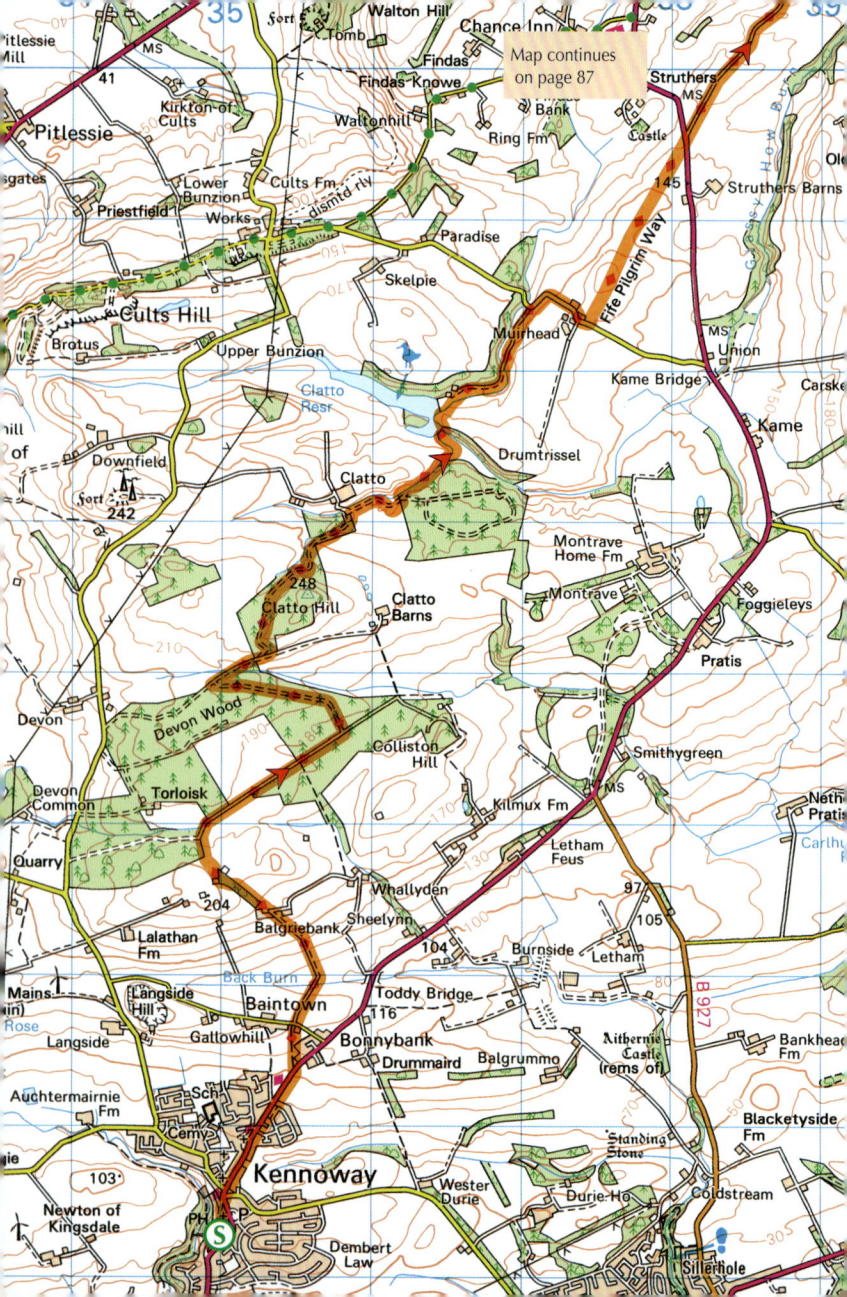

STAGE 5 – KENNOWAY TO CERES

forest of beech and Scots' Pine fills in around the track. Carefully follow the waymarkers for the next 3km, as you make your way through several plots of plantation forest alternating with reforested areas on the slopes of **Clatto Hill** (**2hr**). These are working forests, so be on the lookout for active logging and moving machinery. ▶

The uphill grade is not particularly steep, but it does carry on for over 2km. Between the plantation trees, look for the restored, native, mixed hardwood forest of beech, oak, and ash. The track becomes a wide logging road as you approach the forest on the top of the hill. Round the crest of a smaller hill, and take a sharp right back along a gravel track for 400m. Follow the waymarkers to the left up through the gate and onto a more overgrown trail. This is the final stretch of the climb up Clatto Hill, with a beautiful grove of larches; the highest point of the FPW at 248m.

Pass through a farm gate you will briefly be crossing into an open cattle area, so beware of livestock. The next 8km are almost all downhill into Ceres. Clatto Den is a hidden and wild glen with a babbling burn that runs to **Clatto Reservoir** (**50min**), a peaceful spot and a hidden gem for wildlife and birds. ▶ After you pass over a small dam, you arrive at a red gravel pathway which you will follow to the foot of the reservoir. A slight uphill takes you away from the reservoir and across over a short bridge, back to a quiet single-track road that winds through peaceful forest on the farm fields for about 1.4km.

At the T-junction head slightly to the right and uphill, then the main road jogs to the left at **Muirhead Farm**. Follow it for 10m to the other side of the cottages and look for the gate on your left, which will bring you into a field. The views open up to beautiful countryside as you walk the Waterless Way, an ancient track travelled by pilgrims for centuries. ▶

The history of conflict between the Church of Scotland and the Roman Catholic Church becomes more visible as you near St Andrews, where the

---

Note: some waymarkers are confusing or may be changed due to logging operations. Follow all signs.

Clatto Reservoir was created as a water source for the city of Dundee in 1874.

To your left you will see Tarvit Hill and its monument, originally marking the 1559 Treaty of Garlie Bank, when Queen Mary agreed not to attack Cupar. The present monument honours Queen Victoria.

The path follows an old stone wall through farmlands that have been worked for centuries

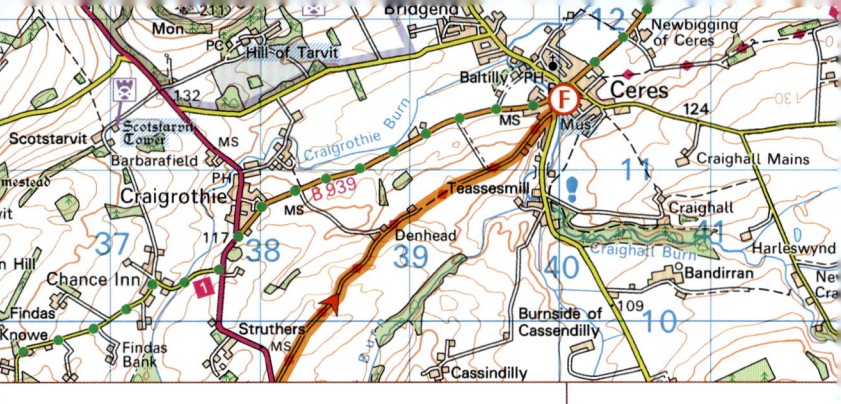

Scottish Reformation started. The Reformation occurred in 1560 in Scotland but religious conflict continued, especially between nobles who vied for power. On 3rd May, 1679, Archbishop of St Andrews, James Sharp, an Episcopalian, travelled from Edinburgh and along the Waterless Way to Ceres. A mob of Covenanters, who advocated for Presbyterianism, pursued and attacked him, as an enemy of the Church of Scotland. He was murdered leaving Ceres, hence the name for 'The Bishop's Bridge', over which the FPW crosses. He was buried at Holy Trinity Church in St Andrews.

Coming to the busy A916, carefully cross and continue along the Waterless Road, through countryside that is not very different than it would have been for pilgrims hundreds of years ago. ▶ Follow the single-track farm road, briefly turning into a grassy path. You can see the church tower and the picturesque town of **Ceres** (**1hr 55min**) off in the distance. Follow Woodburn Road down into the centre of town, where you will see the gateway, public toilets, and the Fife Folk Museum with a cafe.

The **Fife Folk Museum** is well worth a visit, and holds many artifacts from the the region's farming past. The old Weigh House has a very thorough exhibit on weights and measures. Look for the carving above the doorway: 'God Bless the Just' with a symbol for a scale.

You can glimpse Scotstarvit Tower to the left, a fortified tower-house from the 1500s.

CERES

Ceres is one of those rare places that still embodies the scale of a mediaeval village, with its small houses and narrow, often cobbled streets. Ceres is home to the oldest Highland Games in Scotland, which began in 1314, the year of the Battle of Bannockburn, on the return of soldiers from that battle. The games are still held each June, hosted on one of the few remaining village greens in Scotland. It is called 'Bow Butts' because it was used for archery practice. It is possible that the name Ceres is derived from the Roman goddess of agriculture, as for centuries it was an important grain market. However, it is more likely to be derived from the Gaelic word *siar* meaning 'west', as it is the town to the west of St Andrews.

Ceres would have been the last night's stop for pilgrims on their way to St Andrews, and there is some evidence of a hospital and resting house for pilgrims that could have been run by the Culdees in the 1300s. The earliest church records for Ceres link the church here to the Culdee church of St Mary's in St Andrews.

The village of Ceres in the distance

STAGE 6
Ceres to St Andrews

Start	Ceres
Finish	St Andrews
Time	5hr 30min
Distance	16km (10 miles)
Total ascent	170m
Total descent	230m
Gradient	Mostly downhill after Ceres before climbing Ladeddie Hill. The climb is briefly steep, but then levels off before going downhill into St Andrews
Terrain	A mix of grass paths, asphalt and fine gravel trails
Refreshments	Ceres: cafes, small shops, pubs; Craigtoun Country Park: Cafe; St Andrews: grocery, pubs, restaurants, cafes
Toilets	Public toilets in Ceres, Craigtoun Country Park, and St Andrews, behind Holy Trinity Church and at the East Sands and West Sands
Accommodation	Ceres: Hotel, B&B; St Andrews: many hotels, B&Bs

The final stage of the route immerses you in peaceful Fife countryside. After Ceres, there is a long stretch along farm tracks and country roads, as you steadily climb Laddedie Hill. The last half of this stage is a descent into St Andrews, the destination of so many pilgrims past. The walk through the Lade Braes with Kinness Burn bubbling in the background is a peaceful way to end your journey to the beautiful medieval pilgrimage town of St Andrews.

From the FPW gateway in the car park of the Fife Folk Museum, continue over the Bishop's Bridge turning right down Castlegate. Follow the waymarkers past the old cottages. When you reach the top of the lane take an abrupt left. There is no waymarker here, but head towards Schoolhill and you will see a waymarker. Walk to the end of Schoolhill, passing the school. Views of the countryside begin to open up as you follow the footpath at the end of the lane, passing through a gate to meet a long, beech hedgerow. The next 2km of the way bring you through fields, farms, and groves, on alternating footpaths and gravel tracks.

After the second small woodland, look for a fairly obvious waymarker and a small grassy path to your left, heading slightly downhill along the edge of the field. At the bottom of the field pass through the gate and turn right along the farm track as the path levels out. When you meet the B940, follow it for 100m to your left, turn onto the next single-track road on your right, and follow the sign for Kinninmonth. There is a bit of a climb over the next 4km, up Kinninmonth and Laddeddie Hills. Continue through the working farm at Kinninmonth, being respectful and staying on the marked walking path, but ignoring the sign that bars 'unauthorised vehicles'. You will meet an overgrown farm track that continues slightly uphill, gradually growing steeper. Don't forget to look behind you for some stunning views.

Pass over a cattle grid, and enter a livestock area. As you round the crest of **Kinninmonth Hill** (**1hr 30min**), you will be able to see your first glimpse out towards St Andrews Bay and your final destination. After following a single-track road along the side of Ladeddie Hill, the FPW skirts the south side of Drumcarrow Craig. There is a

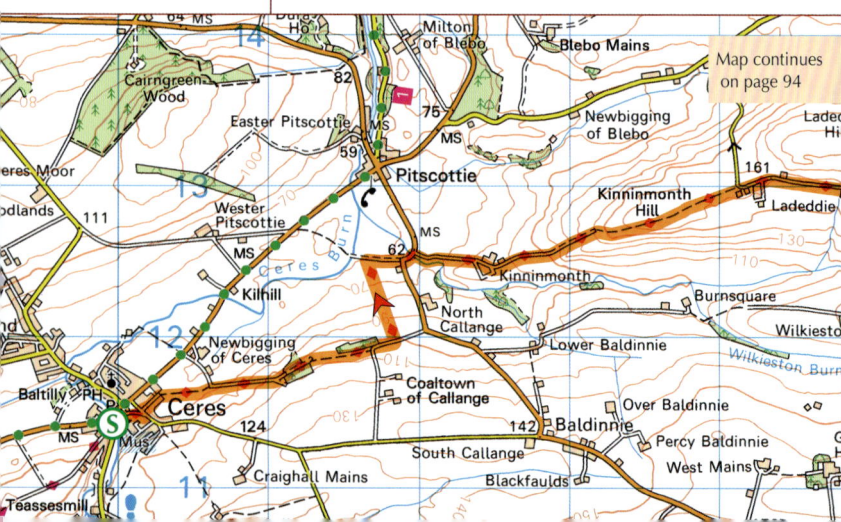

STAGE 6 – CERES TO ST ANDREWS

steep path of 650m up to the top if you would like to see the view and explore the remnants of an Iron Age broch, or defensive house. There are also hut circles, possibly Iron Age houses with a hearth. After passing Drumcarrow Craig, there is a short section of busier road with no pavement. ▶ Continue straight on the smaller one lane road towards **Denhead**, a gentle downhill through the countryside. Look for a golf course on your right, and then a gateway through the stone wall. It's easy to miss, but there is a waymarker.

Follow the thin dirt path through the mixed forest, keeping the golf course on your right. Keep following the waymarkers and the paved path until you meet the entrance road to **Craigtoun Country Park** (**2hr 15min**). There are signs at the end of the car park that signal the entrance to the park. The paths through the park can be confusing, so follow the waymarkers and the maps. The park was once the estate of the Melville family, and

A quiet road, but still travelled by cars and trucks – be sure to keep an eye out

Views open up to the Eden Estuary, an important ecological site for migrating birds and marine life.

Grand views looking back from the hill you just climbed

> The park is owned by Fife Council and boasts a train, mini golf, nature centre, and even a 'Dutch Village' with a castle, island and boats.

bought by the Younger brewing family in 1901, when it was landscaped with the formal gardens and lakes seen today. ◀ The park is a lovely place for a picnic. There is also a cafe and public toilets. Exit the park towards the southeast corner along Cairnsmill Burn. You will be following this waterway for the next 3km, as it eventually meets Kinness Burn.

After about 1km, cross a small lane. Continue towards Lumbo and Bogward. The path winds gently up and down through a meadow, and although a bit overgrown, it is still clear. Skirting the housing, keep the burn to your right. Cross Bogward Road and continue on the path to the left of a bus stop. Don't miss the small path to your left which brings you up to the Bogward Doocot.

> Tucked behind a humble housing estate sits a rare and ancient **Doocot**, also called a dovecote, or 'dove house'. The beehive-shaped structure dates from the mid-1500s, and was used by monks at the Priory of St Andrews to raise pigeons and doves. The doocot has three courses of stone to prevent rats from climbing up it. In return for providing a safe nesting place, the pigeons provided meat, eggs, and guano for fertiliser. There is even a rotating

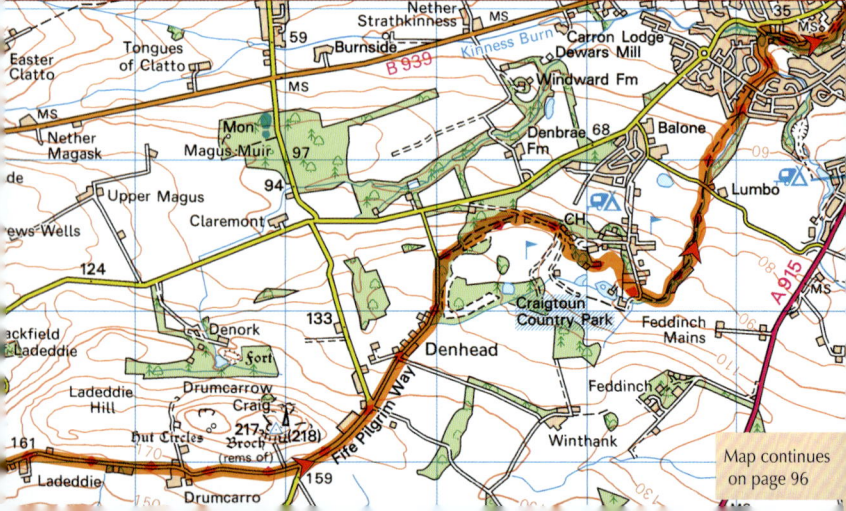

Map continues on page 96

STAGE 6 – CERES TO ST ANDREWS

The path heads through a small forest while following the Cairnsmill Burn

ladder within, to allow access to the roughly 800 nest boxes.

Return to the FPW and turn left to follow the burn. You are now entering the Lade Braes, a forested glen that follows the burn down into the heart of St Andrews. A *lade* is a canal to 'lead' water, and *braes* means hill. You will soon walk past the site of the old mill, and the pond where the water was *lade* to the mill. ▶ The forest becomes deep and dramatic, with many large trees that were planted by John Mackintosh in the late 1800s. Cross over the stone bridge, and turn right to follow the flow of the burn towards the sea.

When you reach a playpark, you'll leave the burn behind you and begin walking into the town of **St Andrews** (**1hr 45min**). Continue to follow Lade Braes Walk, which becomes a pretty little back lane. When you reach Melbourne Place (A 915), take a left and you will meet a busy roundabout. Head through the West Port, on

The Law Mill's roof is pyramid-shaped, and was used as a grain kiln. It is likely that a mill existed in this place for over 800 years, although the present one was built in 1757.

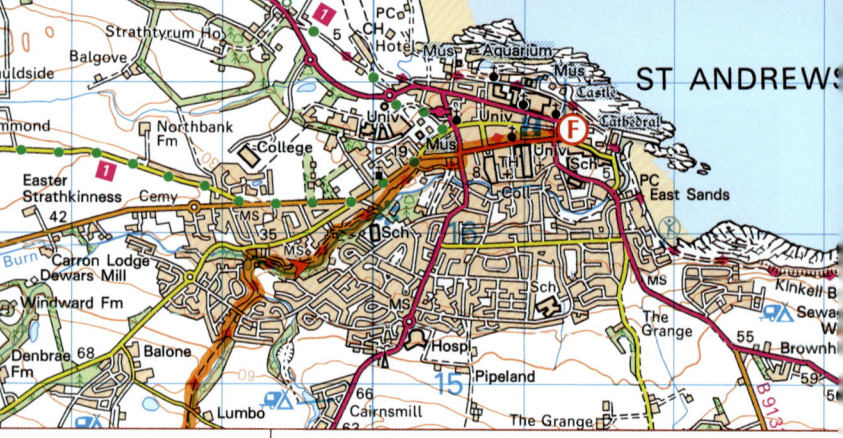

John Knox, regarded as the founder of Presbyterianism, preached at Holy Trinity Church in 1559, fomenting the Protestant Reformation in Scotland.

the east side of the roundabout, which draws you straight down South Street, the pilgrim's final approach to the cathedral. The town of St Andrews itself deserves some lingering, but the end of the Fife Pilgrim Way is located at the cathedral, so continue on. On the left side of South Street, you will see Holy Trinity Church, originally built in 1412, of which the tower dates. ◀ The final FPW gateway marker is located next to the church on Logie's Lane, but you will continue on South Street to the cathedral at the end of the road.

> Prof. Ian Bradley, emeritus professor of Cultural and Spiritual History at University of St Andrews, now hosts **St Margaret's Ecumenical Pilgrimage**, a yearly Good Friday 'walk of witness' through St Andrews, acknowledging the violence done by both Catholics and Protestants during the Reformation.

The main streets of St Andrews remain in their original layout from the 11th century, as processional walkways towards the cathedral and the shrine to St Andrew. Records from the 900s discuss pilgrimages to the shrine, but its popularity peaked between the 14th and 16th centuries. St Andrews Cathedral, the final terminus of the Fife Pilgrim Way, is where the relics of St Andrew once rested. Pilgrims throughout the centuries have walked similar paths to the one you just completed. If you have

STAGE 6 – CERES TO ST ANDREWS

the energy, it is well worth climbing up St Rule's Tower, in the cathedral grounds, to take in a grand view of St Andrews, beaches, and the Fife countryside: an opportunity to reflect on your pilgrim journey.

St Andrews
1. Cathedral
2. Castle
3. St Rule's Tower
4. St Mary's on the Rock
5. All Saints' Chuch
6. Kinburn House Museum
7. Holy Trinity Church/FPW Gateway
8. Tourist Information Centre
9. St Mark's Parish Church
10. St Andrew's Episcopal Church

ST ANDREWS

St Andrews is one of the most historic and picturesque towns in Scotland, which, as a country, sets a high bar. With the oldest golf course in the world, and its miles of sandy beaches, it draws many tourists. There is also a lot of important history to digest. There is a lot to see here, and you may want to take an extra day to explore.

St Andrews Cathedral at the end of the Fife Pilgrim Way

STAGE 6 – CERES TO ST ANDREWS

- St Andrews Cathedral is now mostly in ruins, but it once housed the shrine of St Andrew and was the most important religious centre in Scotland until the Reformation. It was also one of the largest cathedrals in Europe, taking over 150 years to complete. The visitors' centre now holds many of the more fragile stones from the site. The cathedral was torn down during the Scottish Reformation and was mostly destroyed by 1600. Many of the stones were repurposed in other buildings throughout the town. Even though the cathedral is ruined, there is enough of the structure remaining to get a feel for the grandeur of the building which once attracted pilgrims from around Europe. The cathedral grounds are free to enter and tickets for the museum can be purchased at the visitors' centre.
- St Rule's Tower sits within the cathedral grounds and is the oldest structure on site, dating from the 11th century, when it was part of the abbey. It was likely built at the direction of St Margaret to honour St Andrew, and was named for St Regulus, who may have brought St Andrew's relics here. The tower can be climbed by a tiny stone spiral staircase, and offers excellent views on a clear day. Tickets can be purchased in the cathedral visitors' centre.
- The Monk's Well is a holy well located within the cemetery to the south of the cathedral.
- After George Wishart was burned in the streets of St Andrews, Cardinal Beaton was killed when Protestants attacked him in St Andrews Castle in 1546. The castle was then occupied and laid siege to, and tunnels were built into the hard rock beneath. It was destroyed soon after. You still can climb through the tunnels, walk around the castle ruins, and see the shocking conditions of the 'bottle dungeon' for a small entrance fee. There is also an exhibit about the reformation violence that took place here.
- St Andrews University is the oldest university in Scotland, having been founded in the late 15th century to train Catholic clergy. Much of the town is made up of university buildings, many of which are still in use.
- The ruins of the Church of St Mary on the Rock are located just outside of the cathedral walls to the north-east. The church was used by a Culdee community until the 12th century.
- Kinburn House Museum holds a display of pilgrim badges, as well as the original badge that inspired the FPW symbol.

APPENDIX A
Accommodation

Location	Name	Type
Culross	STAY Bed & Breakfast	◯
	The Dundonald Guesthouse and Cottage	◯
	West Fife Pods	◯
Cairneyhill	Forrester Park Resort	◯
Crossford	Keavil House Hotel Best Western Plus	◯
	Adamson Hotel	◯
Dunfermline	The City Hotel	◯
	Auld Mill House Hotel	◯
	Clarke Cottage Guest House	◯
Craigduckie/Loch Fitty	Craigduckie Shepherd Huts	◯
Kinross	The Kirklands Hotel	◯
	The Green Hotel	◯
Leslie	Firbank Lodge	◯
Glenrothes	Holiday Inn Express Glenrothes	◯
	Travelodge Glenrothes	◯
Balfarg	Gilvenbank Hotel	◯
Balbirnie	Balbirnie House	◯
Markinch	Laurel Bank Hotel	◯
	The Fig Tree Markinch	◯

APPENDIX A – ACCOMMODATION

⬢ B&B/guesthouse   ⬢ Self-catering (including pods/glamping)
⬢ Hotel   ⬆ Hostel

Tel	Web/email	Comments
07708 134770	https://stay-culross.com	
07747 044886	https://thedundonald.com	2 night minimum for cottage
07854 175480	www.westfifepods.co.uk	*2.4km off route; 2 pods that sleep 4 people each*
01383 880505	www.forresterparkresort.com	*approx 1km off route*
01383 736258	www.keavilhouse.co.uk	
01383 736132	www.theadamsonhotel.com/	*approx 1km off route*
01383 722538	www.thecityhotel.co.uk	
01383 732152	www.shouthotels.com/auld-mill-house-hotel-dunfermline	
01383 735935	https://www.clarkecottageguesthouse.co.uk	
07855 461930	www.craigduckie.co.uk	*2km off route, path around N of Loch Fitty is shortest route; 2 huts each sleep 4*
01577 863313	https://thekirklandshotel.com	*10km from Kelty via taxi*
01577 863467	www.green-hotel.com	*10km from Kelty via taxi*
07971 176977	https://firbank-lodge.com	
01592 745509	www.ihg.com/holidayinnexpress/hotels/us/en/glenrothes/glnuk/hoteldetail	
08719 846278	www.travelodge.co.uk/hotels/274/Glenrothes-hotel	*4km from path but inexpensive*
01592 742077	https://gilvenbankhotel.co.uk	
01592 610066	https://balbirnie.co.uk	
01592 611205	www.laurelbankhotel.co.uk	
01592 504697	www.thefigtreemarkinch.co.uk	

WALKING THE FIFE PILGRIM WAY

Location	Name	Type
Leven	*The Caledonian Hotel*	🔴
	Lomond Guest House	🔵
Ceres	Meldrums Hotel	🔴
	Craighall Steading	🔵
St Andrews	Premier Inn St Andrews	🔴
Stage 1A		
Edinburgh	*Edinburgh Central Youth Hostel*	⬆
North Queensferry	Northcliff	🟢
	DoubleTree by Hilton Queensferry Crossing	🔴
Rosyth	Hill Park Hotel	🔴
	Three Bridges B&B	🔵

Appendix A – Accommodation

Tel	Web/email	Comments
01333 424101	www.greenekinginns.co.uk/hotels/fife/caledonian-hotel	approx 5km from Kennoway
01333 300511	www.lomondguesthouse.co.uk	approx 5km from Kennoway, offer a secure drying room to dry out walking gear
01334 845800	www.meldrumsceres.co.uk	
07840 903161	www.craighallsteading.co.uk	approx 1.5km off route
03330 035608	www.premierinn.com/gb/en/hotels/scotland/fife/st-andrews/st-andrews.html	many hotels and B&Bs in St Andrews, this was cheapest hotel at time of 2024 publication
01315 242090	www.hostellingscotland.org.uk/hostels/edinburgh-central	tram to Haymarket station then train to Stage 1A start at North Queensferry (45min total)
07771 981966	https://northcliff.co.uk	
01383 410000	https://double-tree-queens-ferry.co.uk	approx 1km from start of route
01383 419977	www.hillparkhotel.co.uk	
01383 419176	www.threebridgesbandb.co.uk	

APPENDIX B
Churches along the FPW

All along the Fife Pilgrim Way, you will encounter ancient churches, whose doors are often open to pilgrims and walkers of any faith or none. These parish churches often hold storied histories and surprising artifacts. Many churches in Scotland were built on pagan holy sites and sacred woodland groves, and Scottish churchyards often hold sacred wells or ancient yew trees, some of which are thousands of years old. We encourage you to stop, rest, and shelter in these churches and their churchyards along the way. It is worth contacting these churches directly and asking if they offer any facilities or even overnight 'champing'.

Stages 1 and 1A: Culross/North Queensferry to Dunfermline
Cairneyhill Parish Church
www.cairneyhillchurch.org.uk

Dunfermline Abbey
https://dunfermlineabbey.com/wwp

St Margaret's Roman Catholic Church
www.stmargaretsdunfermline.co.uk

Viewfield Baptist Church
www.viewfield.org.uk

Holy Trinity Episcopal Church
www.holytrinitychurch.org.uk

Stage 2: Dunfermline to Kelty
Kelty Church
www.keltychurch.co.uk

Stage 3: Kelty to Leslie
Auchterderran and Kinglassie Church of Scotland
www.auchterderrankinglassieparishchurch.org

Stage 4: Leslie to Kennoway
Christ's Kirk Glenrothes
www.christskirk.uk

Markinch and Thornton Parish Church
www.markinchchurch.org.uk

St Kenneth's Kennoway Parish Church
www.stkenneths.org.uk

Stage 5: Kennoway to Ceres
Ceres Church of Scotland
www.ckschurch.org

Stage 6: Ceres to St Andrews
Holy Trinity Church of Scotland
www.holyt.co.uk

St Mark's Church of Scotland
www.stmarksparishchurch.org

St Andrew's Episcopal Church
www.stasstas.com

All Saints' Episcopal Church
www.allsaints-standrews.org.uk

APPENDIX C
Useful contacts

Emergency number
Tel 999

People and organisations
The Pilgrim Pastor
www.fifecoastandcountrysidetrust.co.uk/projects/the-pilgrim-pastor

Fife Coast & Countryside Trust
www.fifecoastandcountrysidetrust.co.uk

The British Pilgrimage Trust
www.britishpilgrimage.org

Weather forecasts
www.metoffice.gov.uk
www.bbc.co.uk/weather

Museums and attractions
Culross
Palace and Garden
www.nts.org.uk/visit/places/culross

Dunfermline
Dunfermline Abbey
www.historicenvironment.scot/visit-a-place/places/dunfermline-abbey-and-palace

Carnegie Birthplace Museum
www.carnegiebirthplace.com

Carnegie Library and Galleries
www.visitscotland.com/info/see-do/dunfermline-carnegie-library-and-galleries-p1423451

St Margaret's Cave
www.onfife.com/venues/st-margarets-cave

Dunfermline Museum
www.onfife.com/museum

Lochore Meadows
www.lochoremeadows.org

Ceres
Fife Folk Museum
www.fifefolkmuseum.org

Craigtoun Country Park
www.friendsofcraigtoun.org.uk

St Andrews
St Andrews Information Centre
70 Market St, KY16 9NU
Tel 01334 472021

St Andrews Cathedral
www.historicenvironment.scot/visit-a-place/places/st-andrews-cathedral

St Andrews Castle
www.historicenvironment.scot/visit-a-place/places/st-andrews-castle

St Andrews Museum
www.onfife.com/venues/st-andrews-museum

St Andrews Heritage Museum and Garden
www.standrewsmuseum.com

Wardlaw Museum at University of St Andrews

Walking the Fife Pilgrim Way

www.st-andrews.ac.uk/museums/visit-us/wardlaw

R&A World Golf Museum
www.worldgolfmuseum.com

Transport
Traveline
Tel 0871 200 22 33
www.travelinescotland.com

Fife Council
www.fifedirect.org.uk

Buses
Stagecoach
www.stagecoachbus.com

Trains
ScotRail
www.scotrail.co.uk

Closest stations to the Fife Pilgrim Way:

- North Queensferry
- Inverkeithing
- Dunfermline Town
- Dunfermline Queen Margaret
- Cowdenbeath
- Markinch
- Leuchars (for St Andrews)

Taxis
There are dozens of local taxi companies. The best option might be to ask for the number of the local one in a shop.

For a list of Fife cab companies and their phone numbers:
www.taxipricecompare.co.uk/directory/browse/fife/?county=fife

APPENDIX D
Further reading

Bradley, Ian. (2019) *The Fife Pilgrim Way: In the footsteps of monks, miners and martyrs.* Birlinn: Edinburgh, UK

Bradley, Ian. (2020). *Following the Celtic Way: a new assessment of Celtic Christianity.* Augsburg Books, Augsburg, Germany

Dove, Giles. (1988). *'Saints, Dedications and cults in medieval Fife'* MPhil thesis, University of St Andrews

Lines, Marianna. (2014). *The traveller's guide to sacred Scotland: a guide to Scotland's ancient sites and sacred places.* Gothic Image Publications: Glastonbury, UK

MacQuarrie, Alan. (1997). *The saints of Scotland.* John Donald: Edinburgh, UK

Mayhew-Smith, Nick and Hayward, Guy. (2020). *Britain's pilgrim places.* Lifestyle Press Ltd: London, UK

Omand, Donald (ed.) (2000). *The Fife book.* Birlinn: Edinburgh, UK

Turpie, Tom. (2016). *'Fife Pilgrim Way: report detailing historical references to pilgrimage and the Cult of the Saints in Fife'* Available online: https://dunfgpr.stir.ac.uk/fife-pilgrim-way

Maps
Ordnance Survey Map 367 Dunfermline, Kirkcaldy & Glenrothes South
https://shop.ordnancesurvey.co.uk/map-of-dunfermline-kirkcaldy-glenrothes-south

Ordnance Survey Map 370 Glenrothes North, Falkland & Lomond Hills
https://shop.ordnancesurvey.co.uk/map-of-glenrothes-north-falkland-lomond-hills

Ordnance Survey Map 371 St Andrews & East Fife
https://shop.ordnancesurvey.co.uk/map-of-st-andrews-east-fife

Fife Pilgrim Way Footprint Map
www.cordee.co.uk/CWN497.php

DOWNLOAD THE ROUTES IN GPX FORMAT

All the routes in this guide are available for download from:

www.cicerone.co.uk/1224/GPX

as standard format GPX files. You should be able to load them into most online GPX systems and mobile devices, whether GPS or smartphone. You may need to convert the file into your preferred format using a conversion programme such as gpsvisualizer.com or one of the many other such websites and programmes.

When you follow this link, you will be asked for your email address and where you purchased the guidebook, and have the option to subscribe to the Cicerone e-newsletter.

www.cicerone.co.uk

LISTING OF CICERONE GUIDES

BRITISH ISLES CHALLENGES, COLLECTIONS AND ACTIVITIES
Great Walks on the England Coast Path
Map and Compass
The Big Rounds
The Book of the Bivvy
The Book of the Bothy
The Mountains of England and Wales:
  Vol 1 Wales
  Vol 2 England
The National Trails
Walking the End to End Trail

SHORT WALKS SERIES
Short Walks Hadrian's Wall
Short Walks Lake District — Keswick, Borrowdale and Buttermere
Short Walks Lake District — Windermere Ambleside and Grasmere
Short Walks Lake District — Coniston and Langdale
Short Walks in Arnside and Silverdale
Short Walks in Nidderdale
Short Walks in Northumberland: Wooler, Rothbury, Alnwick and the coast
Short Walks on the Malvern Hills
Short Walks in Cornwall: Falmouth and the Lizard
Short Walks in Cornwall: Land's End and Penzance
Short Walks in the South Downs: Brighton, Eastbourne and Arundel
Short Walks in the Surrey Hills
Short Walks on Dartmoor — South: Ivybridge and Princetown
Short Walks on Exmoor
Short Walks Winchester
Short Walks in Pembrokeshire: Tenby and the south
Short Walks in Dumfries and Galloway
Short Walks on the Isle of Mull
Short Walks on the Orkney Islands
Short Walks on the Shetland Islands

SCOTLAND
Ben Nevis and Glen Coe
Cycling in the Hebrides
Cycling the North Coast 500
Great Mountain Days in Scotland
Mountain Biking in Southern and Central Scotland
Mountain Biking in West and North West Scotland
Not the West Highland Way
Scotland
Scotland's Best Small Mountains
Scotland's Mountain Ridges
Scottish Wild Country Backpacking
Skye's Cuillin Ridge Traverse
The Borders Abbeys Way
The Great Glen Way
The Great Glen Way Map Booklet
The Hebridean Way
The Hebrides
The Isle of Mull
The Isle of Skye
The Skye Trail
The Southern Upland Way
The West Highland Way
Walking Ben Lawers, Rannoch and Atholl
Walking in the Cairngorms
Walking in the Pentland Hills
Walking in the Scottish Borders
Walking in the Southern Uplands
Walking in Torridon, Fisherfield, Fannichs and An Teallach
Walking Loch Lomond and the Trossachs
Walking on Arran
Walking on Harris and Lewis
Walking on Jura, Islay and Colonsay
Walking on Rum and the Small Isles
Walking on the Orkney and Shetland Isles
Walking on Uist and Barra
Walking the Cape Wrath Trail
Walking the Corbetts Vol 1 South of the Great Glen
Walking the Corbetts Vol 2 North of the Great Glen
Walking the Fife Pilgrim Way
Walking the Galloway Hills
Walking the John o' Groats Trail
Walking the Munros
  Vol 1 — Southern, Central and Western Highlands
  Vol 2 — Northern Highlands and the Cairngorms
Walking the West Highland Way
West Highland Way Map Booklet
Winter Climbs in the Cairngorms
Winter Climbs: Ben Nevis and Glen Coe

NORTHERN ENGLAND ROUTES
Cycling the Reivers Route
Cycling the Way of the Roses
Hadrian's Cycleway
Hadrian's Wall Path
Hadrian's Wall Path Map Booklet
The Coast to Coast Cycle Route
The Coast to Coast Map Booklet
The Coast to Coast Walk
The Pennine Way
Pennine Way Map Booklet
Walking the Dales Way
The Dales Way Map Booklet

LAKE DISTRICT
Bikepacking in the Lake District
Cycling in the Lake District
Great Mountain Days in the Lake District
Joss Naylor's Lakes, Meres and Waters of the Lake District
Lake District Winter Climbs
Lake District: High Level and Fell Walks
Lake District: Low Level and Lake Walks
Mountain Biking in the Lake District
Outdoor Adventures with Children — Lake District
Scrambles in the Lake District —
  North
  South
Trail and Fell Running in the Lake District
Walking The Cumbria Way
Walking the Lake District Fells —
  Borrowdale
  Buttermere
  Coniston
  Keswick
  Langdale
  Mardale and the Far East
  Patterdale
  Wasdale
Walking the Tour of the Lake District

NORTH-WEST ENGLAND AND THE ISLE OF MAN
Cycling the Pennine Bridleway
Isle of Man Coastal Path
The Lancashire Cycleway
The Lune Valley and Howgills
Walking in Cumbria's Eden Valley
Walking in Lancashire
Walking in the Forest of Bowland and Pendle
Walking on the Isle of Man
Walking on the West Pennine Moors
Walking the Ribble Way
Walks in Silverdale and Arnside

NORTH-EAST ENGLAND, YORKSHIRE DALES AND PENNINES
Cycling in the Yorkshire Dales
Great Mountain Days in the Pennines
Mountain Biking in the Yorkshire Dales
The Cleveland Way and the Yorkshire Wolds Way
The Cleveland Way Map Booklet
The North York Moors
Trail and Fell Running in the Yorkshire Dales
Walking in County Durham

Walking in Northumberland
Walking in the North Pennines
Walking in the Yorkshire Dales:
　North and East
　South and West
Walking St Cuthbert's Way
Walking St Oswald's Way and
　Northumberland Coast Path

DERBYSHIRE, PEAK DISTRICT AND MIDLANDS
Cycling in the Peak District
Dark Peak Walks
Scrambles in the Dark Peak
Walking in Derbyshire
Walking in the Peak District —
　White Peak East
　White Peak West

WALES AND WELSH BORDERS
Cycle Touring in Wales
Cycling Lon Las Cymru
Great Mountain Days in Snowdonia
Hillwalking in Shropshire
Mountain Walking in Snowdonia
Offa's Dyke Path
Offa's Dyke Map Booklet
The Pembrokeshire Coast Path
Pembrokeshire Coast Path Map Booklet
Scrambles in Snowdonia
Snowdonia: 30 Low-level and Easy Walks — North, South
The Cambrian Way
The Snowdonia Way
The Wye Valley Walk
Walking Glyndwr's Way
Walking in Carmarthenshire
Walking in Pembrokeshire
Walking in the Brecon Beacons
Walking in the Wye Valley
Walking on Gower
Walking the Severn Way
Walking the Shropshire Way
Walking the Wales Coast Path

SOUTHERN ENGLAND
20 Classic Sportive Rides in South East England
20 Classic Sportive Rides in South West England
Cycling in the Cotswolds
Mountain Biking on the North Downs
Mountain Biking on the South Downs
The North Downs Way
North Downs Way Map Booklet
Walking the South West Coast Path
South West Coast Path Map Booklet
　— Vol 1: Minehead to St Ives
　— Vol 2: St Ives to Plymouth
　— Vol 3: Plymouth to Poole
Suffolk Coast and Heath Walks
The Cotswold Way
The Cotswold Way Map Booklet
The Kennet and Avon Canal
The Lea Valley Walk
The Peddars Way and Norfolk Coast Path
The Pilgrims' Way
The Ridgeway National Trail
The Ridgeway Map Booklet
The South Downs Way
The South Downs Way Map Booklet
The Thames Path
The Thames Path Map Booklet
The Two Moors Way
Two Moors Way Map Booklet
Walking Hampshire's Test Way
Walking in Cornwall
Walking in Essex
Walking in Kent
Walking in London
Walking in Norfolk
Walking in the Chilterns
Walking in the Cotswolds
Walking in the Isles of Scilly
Walking in the New Forest
Walking in the North Wessex Downs
Walking on Dartmoor
Walking on Guernsey
Walking on Jersey
Walking on the Isle of Wight
Walking the Dartmoor Way
Walking the Jurassic Coast
Walking the Sarsen Way
Walks in the South Downs National Park
Cycling Land's End to John o' Groats

ALPS CROSS-BORDER ROUTES
100 Hut Walks in the Alps
Alpine Ski Mountaineering Vol 1 — Western Alps
The Karnischer Hohenweg
The Tour of the Bernina
Trekking the Tour du Mont Blanc
Tour du Mont Blanc Map Booklet
Trail Running — Chamonix and the Mont Blanc region
Trekking Chamonix to Zermatt
Trekking in the Alps
Trekking in the Silvretta and Ratikon Alps
Trekking Munich to Venice
Walking in the Alps

FRANCE, BELGIUM, AND LUXEMBOURG
Camino de Santiago — Via Podiensis
Chamonix Mountain Adventures
Cycling London to Paris
Cycling the Canal de la Garonne
Cycling the Canal du Midi
Mont Blanc Walks
Mountain Adventures in the Maurienne
Short Treks on Corsica
The Grand Traverse of the Massif Central
The Moselle Cycle Route
Trekking in the Vanoise
Trekking the Cathar Way
Trekking the GR10
Trekking the GR20 Corsica
Trekking the Robert Louis Stevenson Trail
The GR5 Trail
The GR5 Trail —
　Vosges and Jura
　Benelux and Lorraine
Via Ferratas of the French Alps
Walking in Provence — East
Walking in Provence — West
Walking in the Auvergne
Walking in the Briançonnais
Walking in the Dordogne
Walking in the Haute Savoie: North
Walking in the Haute Savoie: South
Walking on Corsica
Walking the Brittany Coast Path
Walking in the Ardennes

PYRENEES AND FRANCE/SPAIN CROSS-BORDER ROUTES
Shorter Treks in the Pyrenees
The Pyrenean Haute Route
The Pyrenees
Trekking the Cami dels Bons Homes
Trekking the GR11 Trail
Walks and Climbs in the Pyrenees

SPAIN AND PORTUGAL
Camino de Santiago: Camino Frances
Costa Blanca Mountain Adventures
Cycling the Camino de Santiago
Mountain Walking in Mallorca
Mountain Walking in Southern Catalunya
Spain's Sendero Historico: The GR1
The Andalucian Coast to Coast Walk
The Camino del Norte and Camino Primitivo
The Camino Ingles and Ruta do Mar
The Mountains Around Nerja
The Mountains of Ronda and Grazalema
The Sierras of Extremadura
Trekking in Mallorca
Trekking in the Canary Islands
Trekking the GR7 in Andalucia
Walking and Trekking in the Sierra Nevada
Walking in Andalucia
Walking in Catalunya —
　Barcelona
　Girona Pyrenees
Walking in the Picos de Europa
Walking La Via de la Plata and Camino Sanabres
Walking on Gran Canaria
Walking on La Gomera and El Hierro
Walking on La Palma
Walking on Lanzarote and Fuerteventura
Walking on Tenerife
Walking on the Costa Blanca
Walking the Camino dos Faros
Portugal's Rota Vicentina

The Camino Portugues
Walking in Portugal
Walking in the Algarve
Walking on Madeira
Walking on the Azores

SWITZERLAND
Switzerland's Jura Crest Trail
The Swiss Alps
Tour of the Jungfrau Region
Trekking the Swiss Via Alpina
Walking in Arolla and Zinal
Walking in the Bernese Oberland — Jungfrau region
Walking in the Engadine — Switzerland
Walking in the Valais
Walking in Ticino
Walking in Zermatt and Saas-Fee

GERMANY
Hiking and Cycling in the Black Forest
The Danube Cycleway Vol 1
The Rhine Cycle Route
The Westweg
Walking in the Bavarian Alps

POLAND, SLOVAKIA, ROMANIA, HUNGARY AND BULGARIA
The Danube Cycleway Vol 2
The High Tatras
The Mountains of Romania

SCANDINAVIA, ICELAND AND GREENLAND
Hiking in Norway — North
Hiking in Norway — South
Trekking the Kungsleden
Trekking in Greenland — The Arctic Circle Trail
Walking and Trekking in Iceland

SLOVENIA, CROATIA, SERBIA, MONTENEGRO AND ALBANIA
Hiking Slovenia's Juliana Trail
Mountain Biking in Slovenia
The Islands of Croatia
The Julian Alps of Slovenia
The Mountains of Montenegro
The Peaks of the Balkans Trail
The Slovene Mountain Trail
Walking in Slovenia: The Karavanke
Walks and Treks in Croatia

ITALY
Alta Via 1 — Trekking in the Dolomites
Alta Via 2 — Trekking in the Dolomites
Day Walks in the Dolomites
Italy's Grande Traversata delle Alpi
Italy's Sibillini National Park
Ski Touring and Snowshoeing in the Dolomites
The Way of St Francis
Trekking Gran Paradiso: Alta Via 2
Trekking in the Apennines
Trekking the Giants' Trail: Alta Via 1 through the Italian Pennine Alps
Via Ferratas of the Italian Dolomites: Vol 1
Vol 2
Walking in Abruzzo
Walking in Italy's Cinque Terre
Walking in Italy's Stelvio National Park
Walking in Sicily
Walking in the Aosta Valley
Walking in the Dolomites
Walking in Tuscany
Walking in Umbria
Walking Lake Como and Maggiore
Walking Lake Garda and Iseo
Walking on the Amalfi Coast
Walking the Via Francigena Pilgrim Route — Part 2
Walking the Via Francigena Pilgrim Route — Part 3
Walks and Treks in the Maritime Alps

IRELAND
The Wild Atlantic Way and Western Ireland
Walking the Kerry Way
Walking the Wicklow Way

EUROPEAN CYCLING
Cycling the Route des Grandes Alpes
Cycling the Ruta Via de la Plata
The Elbe Cycle Route
The River Loire Cycle Route
The River Rhone Cycle Route

INTERNATIONAL CHALLENGES, COLLECTIONS AND ACTIVITIES
Europe's High Points
Walking the Via Francigena Pilgrim Route — Part 1

AUSTRIA
Innsbruck Mountain Adventures
Trekking Austria's Adlerweg
Trekking in Austria's Hohe Tauern
Trekking in Austria's Stubai Alps
Trekking in Austria's Zillertal Alps
Walking in Austria
Walking in the Salzkammergut: the Austrian Lake District

MEDITERRANEAN
The High Mountains of Crete
Trekking in Greece
Walking and Trekking in Zagori
Walking and Trekking on Corfu
Walking on the Greek Islands — the Cyclades
Walking in Cyprus
Walking on Malta

HIMALAYA
8000 metres
Everest: A Trekker's Guide
Trekking in the Karakoram

NORTH AMERICA
Hiking and Cycling the California Missions Trail
The John Muir Trail
The Pacific Crest Trail

SOUTH AMERICA
Aconcagua and the Southern Andes
Hiking and Biking Peru's Inca Trails
Trekking in Torres del Paine

AFRICA
Kilimanjaro
Walking in the Drakensberg
Walks and Scrambles in the Moroccan Anti-Atlas

NEW ZEALAND AND AUSTRALIA
Hiking the Overland Track

CHINA, JAPAN, AND ASIA
Annapurna
Hiking and Trekking in the Japan Alps and Mount Fuji
Hiking in Hong Kong
Japan's Kumano Kodo Pilgrimage
Japan's Kumano Kodo Pilgrimage
Trekking in Bhutan
Trekking in Ladakh
Trekking in Tajikistan
Trekking in the Himalaya

TECHNIQUES
Fastpacking
The Mountain Hut Book

MINI GUIDES
Alpine Flowers
Navigation
Pocket First Aid and Wilderness Medicine

MOUNTAIN LITERATURE
A Walk in the Clouds
Abode of the Gods
Fifty Years of Adventure
The Pennine Way — the Path, the People, the Journey
Unjustifiable Risk?

For full information on all our guides, books and eBooks, visit our website:
www.cicerone.co.uk

CICERONE

Trust Cicerone to guide your next adventure, wherever it may be around the world...

Discover guides for hiking, mountain walking, backpacking, trekking, trail running, cycling and mountain biking, ski touring, climbing and scrambling in Britain, Europe and worldwide.

Connect with Cicerone online and find inspiration.

- buy books and ebooks
- articles, advice and trip reports
- GPX files and updates
- regular newsletter

cicerone.co.uk